CRAVE
MINNEAPOLIS
ST. PAUL

The Urban Girl's Manifesto

Melody Biringer

CRAVE Minneapolis/St. Paul: The Urban Girl's Manifesto

A publication of The CRAVE Company
1805 12th Ave W #A
Seattle WA 98119
206.282.0173

thecravecompany.com/minneapolis
twitter.com/cravemsp
facebook.com/craveminneapolis

While every effort was made to ensure the accuracy of the information, details are subject to change so please call ahead. Neither The CRAVE Company nor CRAVE Minneapolis/St. Paul shall be responsible for any consequences arising from the publication or use.

All editorial content in this publication is the sole opinion of CRAVE Minneapolis/St. Paul and our contributing writers. No fees or services were rendered in exchange for inclusion in this publication.

Printed in the United States of America

ISBN 978-0-9847143-1-5
Second Edition
November 2011
$19.95 USD

The Urban Girl's Manifesto

We CRAVE Community.
At CRAVE Minneapolis/St. Paul we believe in acknowledging, celebrating and passionately supporting local businesses. We know that, when encouraged to thrive, neighborhood establishments enhance communities and provide rich experiences not usually encountered in mass-market. By introducing you to the savvy businesswomen in this guide, we hope that CRAVE Minneapolis/St. Paul will help inspire your own inner entrepreneur.

We CRAVE Adventure.
We could all use a getaway, and at CRAVE Minneapolis/St. Paul we believe that you don't need to be a jet-setter to have a little adventure. There's so much to do and explore right in your own backyard. We encourage you to break your routine, to venture away from your regular haunts, to visit new businesses, to explore all the funky finds and surprising spots that the Twin Cities have to offer. Whether it's to hunt for a birthday gift, indulge in a spa treatment, order a bouquet of flowers or connect with like-minded people, let CRAVE Minneapolis/St. Paul be your guide for a one-of-a-kind hometown adventure.

We CRAVE Quality.
CRAVE Minneapolis/St. Paul is all about quality products and thoughtful service. We know that a satisfying shopping trip requires more than a simple exchange of money for goods, and that a rejuvenating spa date entails more than a quick clip of the cuticles and a swipe of polish. We know you want to come away feeling uplifted, beautiful, excited, relaxed, relieved and, above all, knowing you got the most bang for your buck. We have scoured the city to find the hidden gems, new hot spots and old standbys, all with one thing in common: they're the best of the best!

A Guide to Our Guide

CRAVE Minneapolis/St. Paul is more than a guidebook. It's a savvy, quality-of-lifestyle book devoted entirely to local businesses owned by women. CRAVE Minneapolis/St. Paul will direct you to some of the best local spots—top boutiques, spas, cafés, stylists, fitness studios and more. And we'll introduce you to the inspired, dedicated women behind these exceptional enterprises, for whom creativity, quality, innovation and customer service are paramount.

Not only is CRAVE Minneapolis/St. Paul an intelligent guide for those wanting to know what's happening throughout town, it's a directory for those who value the contributions that spirited businesswomen make to our region.

GOLD MEDAL FLOUR

Gold Medal Flour building by Elijah Parker

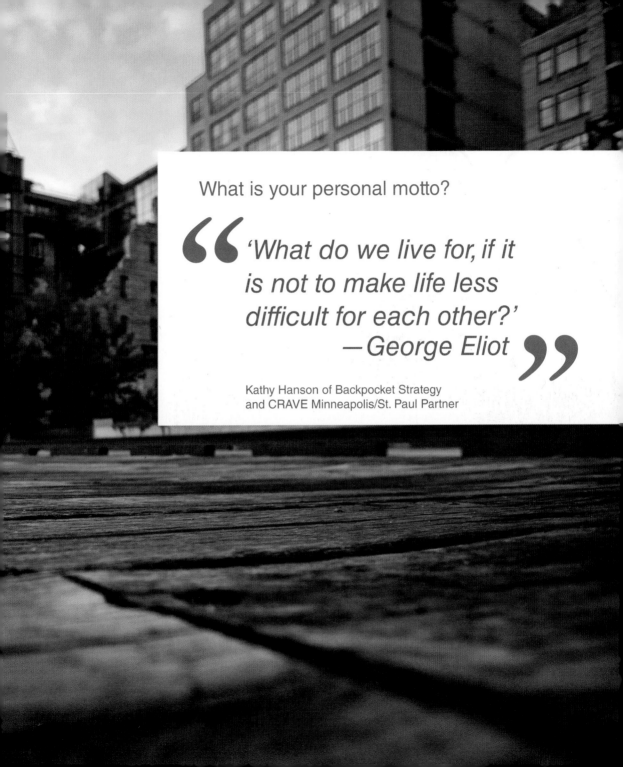

What is your personal motto?

" *'What do we live for, if it is not to make life less difficult for each other?'* —George Eliot "

Kathy Hanson of Backpocket Strategy
and CRAVE Minneapolis/St. Paul Partner

A Gentle Touch by Sandra

5009 Excelsior Blvd, Ste 144, St Louis Park, 952.926.3928

Attentive. Accomplished. Peaceful.
For more than 15 years, A Gentle Touch by Sandra has satisfied clients of all ages who want personal, attentive beauty enhancements in a private setting. Known for creating a peaceful and relaxing atmosphere, Sandra applies her keen expertise for waxing and precisely shaping eyebrows, as well as offering a variety of esthetic services and soothing facial treatments. Personal care and affordability keep clients totally satisfied.

Photos by Giliane E. Mansfeldt Photography

Q&A

What makes your business unique?
Exceptional service. My expert waxing
techniques and relaxing facials are
given in a quiet, cozy setting.

What advice would you give women
who are starting a business?
Make sure you have a passion for success
and for what you want to do. Never
doubt your ability to be successful.

What is the biggest perk about
owning a small business?
While running my own business certainly
keeps me busy, I appreciate the feeling
of personal freedom and flexibility
that comes from being my own boss.
The empowerment is wonderful!

What is your biggest motivator?
The desire to remain successful; to me
this means the ability to keep building
wonderful relationships with my clients
while providing the services they enjoy
and that make them feel beautiful.

What is your personal motto?
Exceptionalism in every aspect of life.

What do you CRAVE?
Health, prosperity, happiness and chocolate!

Sandra Caldwell

Aagesen Chiropractic Clinic

5050 West 36th St, Ste 100, St Louis Park, 612.920.1092
aagesenchiro.com, Twitter: @AagesenChiro

Holistic. Healing. Compassionate.
Aagesen Chiropractic Clinic has been practicing chiropractic care and natural healing since 1988. This beautiful, spa-like wellness clinic offers patients a lifetime of good health through chiropractic, massage, acupuncture, physical and occupational therapy. Aagesen Chiropractic is a five-star clinic. They enjoy educating their patients on better health. Everyone from babies to seniors benefits from the natural health care at Aagesen Chiropractic.

Dr. Maria Aagesen-Reznecheck

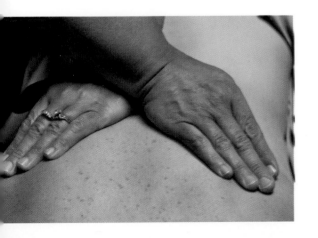

Q&A

What makes your business unique?
Aagesen Chiropractic integrates many holistic services in each treatment. Our goal is to understand the unique symptoms of each patient, heal their bodies and nurture their spirits.

What would you like customers to know about your business?
Our clinic not only offers chiropractic care and massage therapy, but we also provide craniosacral therapy, myofasical release and nutritional counseling to help all patients achieve optimal health and wellness.

What is your biggest motivator?
My family and children are my biggest motivators. I want them to know that with hard work, a creative spirit and determination, success is achievable.

What is your personal motto?
Life is truly a blessing. Enjoy each day and be grateful for the many things that are easy to take for granted.

13

Shelley Conn

Q&A

What makes your business unique?
Few Twin Cities acupuncturists practice cosmetic acupuncture. Trained and certified in the Mei Zen method of cosmetic acupuncture, I focus on facial points that pull out wrinkles, plump and lift.

What is your favorite part of being an entrepreneur?
That I can take as much time as I need to help a client.

Who is your role model or mentor?
My grandfather taught me how to have a good sense of humor and have fun with everything.

What is your personal motto?
People don't care how much you know until they know how much you care.

What do you CRAVE?
Good health, olives and dark chocolate.

Acupuncture in the Park

5821 Cedar Lake Rd, St Louis Park, 952.545.2250
acupunctureinthepark.com

Rejuvenating. Calming. Natural.
At Acupuncture in the Park, Shelley Conn focuses on women's health and beauty using cosmetic acupuncture. After repeated treatments, the face glows, fine lines decrease, wrinkles soften, and eye puffiness diminishes while the face and jowls are lifted. A healthy alternative to Botox and surgery, cosmetic acupuncture unveils natural beauty from the inside out!

Amy Zaroff

Q&A

What would you like customers to know about your business?
From party etiquette to thank you notes, each detail is handled with care and nothing is overlooked. Amy Zaroff Events + Design treats every service as a special service—every time.

What is your favorite part of being an entrepreneur?
The freedom to make change and be nimble. There is no such thing as a five-year plan anymore. I love the ability to innovate and create constant excitement.

Who is your role model or mentor?
My father. He is passionate and kind and deeply cares for others. Everyday he makes it a priority to help someone in need and often it is done anonymously.

Amy Zaroff
Events + Design

7179 Washington Ave S, Edina, 952.941.3371
amyzaroff.com, Twitter: @amyzaroff

Perceptive. Visionary. Authentic.
As a former television producer and restauranteur, everything Amy Zaroff has done in her career has been focused on producing incredible experiences and making memories. Amy Zaroff Events + Design is in the business of creating life's most memorable events. As designers and producers, they create distinct event stories through a process that brings your vision to reality.

Ann Eliason and Jackie Weeks

Q&A

What makes your business unique?
The sheer quantity and quality
of merchandise is unmatched
in the Twin Cities.

What would you like customers to
know about your business?
The inventory is constantly changing since
we are buying new pieces everyday. We
have unbeatable diamond prices. We have
vintage mountings available for remounting.
We bring New York fashion to Minnesota.

What advice would you give women
who are starting a business?
Don't start your business hoping to be
the biggest and best... start with your
focus on working harder than anyone else
and you will be far more successful.

Ann and Jack's Vintage Jewelry

1014 Main St, Hopkins, 952.938.4220
annandjacks.com

Ever-changing. Experienced. Unconventional.
This dynamic duo travels the country to bring back fabulous vintage jewelry, fashion to fine, at affordable prices. Along with carrying one of the largest vintage engagement ring selections around—couples flock to find their one-of-a-kind diamond rings—Ann and Jackie are buying vintage costume, sterling and gold jewelry daily. You never know what you might find!

Photos by B Johnson Photos

Annie Ballantine Designs

651.472.3518
annieballantine.com

Warm. Stylish. Affordable.
Annie Ballantine Designs is a full-service interior design studio specializing in affordable design services for residential clients. Annie and her staff will ensure that the design process is fun, enjoyable and never stressful, so you can relax and enjoy the transformation. Services are always tailored to meet client needs. Annie was selected to decorate the White House for the holidays in 2011.

Annie Ballantine

Q&A

What makes your business unique?
I believe that interior design is a necessity, not a luxury. All of my services are priced so that they are affordable for a wide variety of clientele.

What can't you simply live without in your business?
Chic shoes, roomy tote bags, stacks of shelter magazines and a good tape measure!

What is your biggest motivator?
When I finish a project and know that the client's life has improved due to the space we have designed together. This makes the day-to-day stresses worth it!

What do you CRAVE?
Good design is about living a comfortable life. In life, I crave a soft bed, fabulous art, soft music and gorgeous letterpress cards.

Art of Optiks

747 E Lake St, Wayzata, 952.404.2020
artofoptiks.com

Modern. Unique. Advanced.
Art of Optiks is a purveyor of unique eyewear and advanced eye care in
Wayzata, Minn. They have been providing outstanding customer service,
amazing, cutting-edge eye exams, and outstanding eyewear for 10 years.

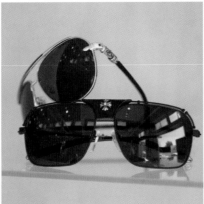

Stephanie Haenes

Q&A

What would you like customers to
know about your business?
We put the customer first. Excellent
customer service is the foundation of our
business and state-of-the art products
and services are the cornerstone.

What is your favorite part of
being an entrepreneur?
I love being in charge of my own
destiny. Knowing that I hold the keys
to my future is very empowering.

What advice would you give women
who are starting a business?
Have a rainy day fund.

What is your biggest motivator?
My desire to always be the best at what I do.

What do you CRAVE?
I crave quiet and mindfulness in my daily life.

B Johnson Photos

612.618.2022
bjohnsonphotos.com, Twitter: @bjohnsondesign

Energetic. Fearless. Professional.
Brenda has the ability to freeze-frame beauty in motion—she's captured everything from the mossy cobblestones of Via Santo Stefano, to mouthwatering cheeseburgers, to beautiful, cozy interiors... and everything in between. Brenda's passion lies in the area of destination, food and fine art photography, but her professional photography services cover the complete spectrum of professional photography needs.

Photos by B Johnson Photos

Brenda Johnson

Q&A

What makes your business unique?
My 20+ years in the commercial advertising and graphic design business, and the understanding that the uniqueness of an image plays a major role in keeping clients satisfied.

What can't you simply live without in your business?
My camera, dark chocolate, and a glass (bottle!) of thick, full-bodied red wine.

What is the best advice you've been given?
Be tenacious. Never burn bridges. Keep your eye on the goal.

What is your biggest motivator?
The excitement and challenge of the next assignment... how will I compose the next perfect shot?

Darya Lucas

Q&A

What would you like customers to know about your business?
Our selection of clothing, shoes and accessories can't be beat. We also carry many brands that are organic and made in America—some are even made here in Minnesota.

What can't you simply live without in your business?
Fishing line for all of our eye-catching window displays, Pandora for some great tunes, and a camera for snapping photos of kids wearing Baby Banou items in the shop.

What is your biggest motivator?
Finding a way to be both happy and successful, while contributing to my community.

Baby Banou

792 Grand Ave, St Paul, 651.340.0062
babybanou.com, Twitter: @babybanou

Adorable. Charming. Unique.
Baby Banou is a one-of-a-kind children's clothing boutique that offers
contemporary and traditional styles for infants and toddlers. This Grand Avenue
gem features a remarkable lineup of brands and a variety of styles. Locally
owned and operated, Baby Banou has a knowledgeable staff and welcoming
atmosphere. Customers can peruse the fabulous selection while kids are
enamored with the magnetic boards, fish tanks and pompon chandeliers.

Kathy Hanson

Q&A

What makes your business unique?
My firmly held conviction that every woman can make her business whatever she dreams it can be. I empower my clients to succeed by giving them practical knowledge and tailored pragmatic tools.

What would you like customers to know about your business?
With my insight, you get clarity. With my passion, you get encouragement. With my tools, you create your own success!

What can't you simply live without in your business?
The wonderful *pickupthephoneIneedyounow* women in my life who truly and deeply support one another.

What advice would you give women who are starting a business?
"Don't try to change the haters—you aren't the jackass whisperer."
—Scott Stratten

What is your biggest motivator?
I get to encourage women every day to believe in themselves by telling them what *can* happen, not what cannot happen.

Backpocket Strategy

952.451.0658
backpocket.biz, Twitter: @backpocketbbf

Perceptive. Passionate. Effective
Kathy Hanson of Backpocket Strategy has mentored and coached entrepreneurs
all over the country to guide their businesses to the next level. Armed with
an MBA and years of experience working with Fortune 100 companies, she
successfully ventured out on her own, gaining national TV and press coverage.
Kathy brings a clear-eyed view with real world practicality to her clients. Kathy is
the secret weapon you just have to have in your back pocket. Pun intended!

The Bee Cottage

441 Second St, Excelsior, 612.454.0030
shopthebeecottage.com

Surprising. Charming. Inspiring.
Nestled in the heart of Excelsior on the banks of Lake Minnetonka, The Bee Cottage
delights the senses with their monthly mix of old and new, vintage, repurposed,
and flea market finds that are guaranteed to decorate your home in a delightful
fashion. You will be inspired by the fresh and imaginative themes in each room of
this quaint, historic house. The Bee Cottage is open just one weekend a month.

Q&A

What would you like customers to know about your business?
Our sales are held the second Wednesday through the following Saturday of each month, 9 a.m.–5 p.m. daily. We are also open on Sundays and Thursday evenings during warmer months. Check our Facebook page often for additional dates over holidays and for citywide events!

What or who inspires you?
Window displays at Ladurée, Isle sur la Sorgue flea market, and the wonderful, creative vendors and artisans who sell their goods at my shop.

What do you CRAVE?
Cane back chairs, gilt mirrors, pistachio macarons, Veuve Clicquot, a morning peek on dailymail.co.uk, and the beauty and tranquility of my childhood home on the farm.

Jennifer Finlay

Q&A

What can't you simply live without in your business?
My sister, a knife and the sewing machine.

What is the best advice you've been given?
Stay true to your designs and don't undervalue yourselves.

What is your biggest motivator?
Having our bags mistaken for other high-end designers and trying to fulfill our endless sketchbook of ideas.

What or who inspires you?
The Austrian annual event Almabtrieb, an alpine fall festival, is a tradition of parading cows from the mountains to the village for winter. Each cow is lavishly adorned with colorful headdresses and bells. We were inspired by the vibrant palette and realized we could put a stylish twist on this unforgettable experience.

Jennifer Wight and Julie Driscoll

Belle Vache

952.461.1918
mysisterandiinc.com

Magnifique. Irresistible. Exquisite.
Belle Vache, French for "beautiful cow," and Furbellish are stunning collections
made with 100 percent genuine leather and fur. Designers Jennifer and
Julie carefully select the finest patent leather, hair-on cowhide, exotic
skin and genuine fur for their handcrafted collections made in Minnesota.
Each original bag, tote and accessory is a remarkable work of art inspired
by the authentic beauty and variations of the natural materials.

Bespoke Hair Artisans

3918 W 49 1/2 St, Edina, 952.224.4062
bespokehairartisans.com, Twitter: @BespokeHA

Luxurious. Approachable. Inspiring.
Bespoke Hair Artisans is inspired by the English tradition of bespoke tailoring, creating custom-made, one-of-a-kind style created for each individual. They are a full-service, boutique salon with a relaxing and inspiring setting. They look, listen and then craft a look that suits the individual and heightens the natural beauty that every person possesses.

Q&A

What makes your business unique?
What makes our business unique is
the technical talent and experience of
our team, our attention to every detail
and our luxurious atmosphere.

**What is your favorite part of
being an entrepreneur?**
Seeing our vision come alive. Creating
insanely great experiences for our guests.
Unlocking our team's creative potential and
fostering an environment that encourages
innovation and allows it to flourish.

What is your personal motto?
There is no assembly line for individuality
and no templates for style. No one
look fits all. Beauty is not off the rack.
Personal style is our passion.

Lisa Williams and Margaret Menke Ayache

Bibelot

1082 Grand Ave, St Paul, 651.222.0321
2276 Como Ave, St Paul, 651.646.5651
4315 Upton Ave S, Minneapolis, 612.925.3175
300 E Hennepin Ave, Minneapolis, 612.379.9300
bibelotshops.com

Inspired. Imaginative. Irresistible.
Bibelot offers a wide-ranging collection of all things delightful: fun and functional gifts, women's clothing, jewelry, toys, stationery and home accents, all thoughtfully chosen and artfully displayed. Whenever possible, emphasis is placed on selecting products that are locally made and designed. Always fresh and current, Bibelot has been delighting customers for 45 years, leading the way in Twin Cities retail.

Photos by Shannon Tacheny of Feather Blue Studios

Roxy Freese

Q&A

What is your favorite part of being an entrepreneur?
Being able to contribute to the larger community has been a priority for me as an entrepreneur; I love knowing that Bibelot is making a significant difference in a variety of ways.

What is your biggest motivator?
My initial motivation was to create a job that incorporated my interests and skills. Continuing motivation comes in offering my staff similar opportunities, and in exciting and serving Bibelot customers.

What or who inspires you?
I am grateful for all that has been. Working with Bibelot's talented and dedicated staff, who strive for excellence every day, continues to inspire and bring me joy.

Denise Alden

Q&A

What makes your business unique?
We carry designer lines that are not found anywhere else in the Twin Cities. Our mission is to show you how fabulous you are!

What would you like customers to know about your business?
You'll be pleasantly surprised when shopping at Bombshell. Instead of finding one piece that sort of works, you'll have to choose between four or five gorgeous, well-made, perfectly fitting outfits!

What do you CRAVE?
Proper gin martinis, French perfume and cabana boys.

Bombshell

794 Grand Ave, St Paul, 651.330.2605
bomb-shell-boutique.com

Glamorous. Vivacious. Inclusive.
Bombshell is for the stylish, sophisticated woman who wears a size 14 to 24.
Located on Grand Avenue in St. Paul, the boutique has clothing for cocktail
parties, brunch with the girls and, of course, date nights. Bombshell offers warm,
personal service in a luxurious environment and was highlighted as one of the
best plus-size boutiques in the country by *Lucky* magazine in July 2011.

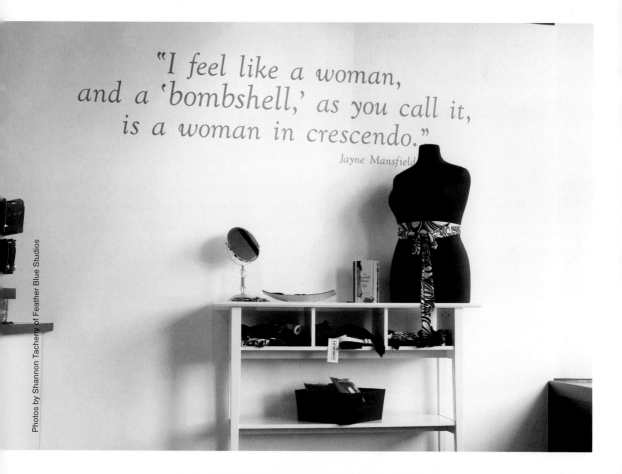

"I feel like a woman,
and a 'bombshell,' as you call it,
is a woman in crescendo."

Jayne Mansfield

Photos by Shannon Tacheny of Feather Blue Studios

Nancy Anderson

Q&A

What makes your business unique?
Calhoun Bikes is a landmark destination, located in Uptown for more than 30 years. We are located one block from the Chain of Lakes and hundreds of miles of bike paths.

What would you like customers to know about your business?
We were the first to offer bike tours of the Twin Cities area. We are a locally owned, family business that promotes biking as a healthy, fun family activity for all ages.

What can't you simply live without in your business?
New specialized bikes. We have a great location in Uptown close to the Midtown Greenway.

What is your personal motto?
Live large and embrace adventure.

Calhoun Bike Tours and Rental

1622 W Lake St, Minneapolis, 612.827.3281
calhounrental.com, Twitter: @ridempls

Funky. Safe. Adventurous.
You've never experienced Minneapolis like this! Discover why Minneapolis was selected "Best Biking City in the USA" by *Bicycling* magazine as you pedal the bike trails of this beautiful city. A Calhoun Bike Tour is the perfect activity for a family reunion, corporate event or convention activity. Whether you're team building or just enjoying a family day, they'll design the perfect bike tour to suit your needs.

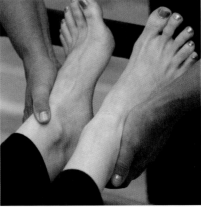

Q&A

What makes your business unique?
As we age, we need a different kind of movement. Centerspace Pilates Studio provides a friendly community of like-minded people who are interested in living a long, healthy life.

What would you like customers to know about your business?
In 10 sessions you will feel the difference, in 20 sessions you will see the difference and in 30 sessions you will have a new body.

What is your favorite part of being an entrepreneur?
Creative freedom.

What or who inspires you?
Travel.

Nancy Anderson

Centerspace Pilates

3302 W 44th St, Minneapolis, 612.822.4776
centerspacepilates.com, Twitter: @centerspacemn

Friendly. Informative. Fun.
Joseph Pilates once said, "You are as young as your spine is flexible." Centerspace Pilates offers a variety of movement enhancing programs. Their monthly workshops teach practical information about exercise, health and lifestyle that improve the quality of everyday life. Exercise is the most effective anti-aging antidote and emotional tonic ever discovered. Centerspace Pilates Studio is conveniently located in beautiful Linden Hills, on the border of Minneapolis and Edina.

Cocoa & Fig

651 Nicollet Mall (Gaviidae Common, Skyway Level, Saks Wing), Minneapolis, 612.333.1485
cocoaandfig.com, Twitter: @cocoaandfig

Tasty. Fresh. Beautiful.
Cocoa & Fig creates delicious and eye-catching dessert designs. Their Gaviidae Common
store provides an array of sweet treats for downtown Minneapolis' most discerning
palettes. In addition, they work individually with clients to create customized desserts for
life's greatest occasions. You can be confident that Cocoa & Fig will create a perfectly
beautiful and delicious addition to your wedding, corporate event or any gathering.

Laurie Pyle

Q&A

What would you like customers to know about your business?
We are passionate about each and every dessert we make. We bake everything from scratch with the best ingredients we can find.

What can't you simply live without in your business?
Butter—everything tastes better with butter!

What is your personal motto?
The greatest blessings come to those who freely give and expect nothing in return.

What do you CRAVE?
To always be challenged—it's what keeps me learning and growing.

Cooks of Crocus Hill

877 Grand Ave, St Paul, 651.228.1333
3925 W 50th St, Edina, 952.285.1903
cooksofcrocushill.com

Authentic. Experiential. Vibrant.
Cooks of Crocus Hill is a locally owned, independent culinary educator and retailer. They
have two cooking schools and two retail stores well stocked with culinary equipment,
kitchen tools, books and packaged food. Their environments are grounded in creating
and sharing authentic culinary experiences, because "Life Happens in the Kitchen!"

Marie Dwyer

 Q&A

What makes your business unique?
We offer cooking classes, culinary
events and interesting culinary tools.

What would you like customers to
know about your business?
We test, taste or sample everything
we offer in our stores. Everything.

Who is your role model or mentor?
Martha Kaemmer. Her passion for
sharing the culinary experience
has a hand in all our work.

What do you CRAVE?
A consistent sense of wellbeing
and a manicure that won't chip.

Traci Nelson

Q&A

What makes your business unique?
Showcasing exceptional products from small companies in France, there are treasures to fit everyone's style. Coquette is open one four-day weekend per month, allowing time to scout fabulous new additions. We are also available by appointment.

What would you like customers to know about your business?
This is a destination shop located on the Lakeville/Elko border. Coquette is open the first Thursday through Sunday of each month. See the Coquette website for the most up-to-date information.

What is your biggest motivator?
The thrill of the hunt! The challenge of finding interesting objects to delight customers, getting them to my shop and displaying them in creative ways is exhilarating.

Coquette: French Style

8920 250th St E, Elko New Market, 612.270.6081
coquettemn.wordpress.com, Twitter: @Coquettemn

Charmant. Authentique. Romantique.
If you crave unique, quality gifts, Coquette is your destination! Gather your
friends and make the trip to this charming, ever-changing boutique. Featuring
French specialties, including gourmet foods, jewelry, art and home decor—
there is something for everyone. Many items cannot be found anywhere
else in the US! You have your own style. Find your inspiration here.

Photos by Gillane E. Manshot Photography

Como Park Conservatory by Shannon Tacheny of Feather Blue Studios

What is the best advice you've been given?

" *Be bold and confident!* "

Cinda Pfeil of Style-Infused Living

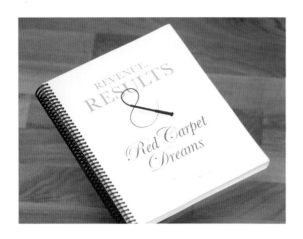

Q&A

What makes your business unique?
I teach women entrepreneurs how
to turn five-figure jobs into six-figure
businesses and six-figure businesses
into seven-figure empires.

What would you like customers to
know about your business?
I'm the author of "Revenue, Results &
Red Carpet Dreams" and the forthcoming
book "Think Like A Stripper: How To
Hustle Your Business Like You Mean It."

What advice would you give women
who are starting a business?
Do The Morning Whip. It will
start your day at 90 mph!

What is the best advice you've been given?
Ask for help.

Who is your role model or mentor?
Kathy Hanson.

What or who inspires you?
I cannot stand to see one more smart,
motivated woman crying in the bathroom
(wrecking her Dior mascara), because
she's not fulfilling her business potential.

Erika Lyremark

Daily Whip

dailywhip.com, Twitter: @dailywhip

Sassy. Inspiring. Motivational.
Erika coaches and inspires smart businesswomen all over the world to empower themselves with her easy-to-follow, hard-to-forget signature 30-day course, The Morning Whip. Every business woman has a superhero inside her—Erika brings her out so you can conquer the world!

Photos by B Johnson Photos

Deirdre Olson

Q&A

What is your biggest motivator?
My customers. I love to hear the stories
about how my jewelry encourages
them or how the gift brought joy to
their daughter, friend or mother.

What is your personal motto?
"Hold fast to your beliefs... respecting
the process as much as the product."
—K. Pabst

What or who inspires you?
An evening at the opera or symphony.
A walk somewhere filled with
beauty. Great song. Beautiful dance.
Essentially, I am inspired when I enjoy
the fruits of others' creativity.

What do you CRAVE?
An afternoon with nowhere to be. Free
time that is truly free nourishes my soul.

Deirdre & Company

612.331.2482
deirdreandcompany.com, Twitter: @DeiandCo

Joyful. Inspirational. Encouraging.
Creating joyful gifts and jewelry celebrating life and faith is the driving passion behind Deirdre & Company. Handmade pieces created in sterling silver, pewter, 14K gold, and colorful glass beads are designed to encourage you and those you love. Client favorites include personalized jewelry and custom logo pieces. Deirdre & Company invites you to experience their collection of simple, unique and stylish pieces.

Design Vertigo

2570 Seventh Ave E, North St Paul, 651.770.1901
designvertigo.net, Twitter: @DesignVertigo1

Inspired. Clever. Refreshing.
Design Vertigo is an inspired shop located just 10 minutes from downtown, in the charming suburb of North Saint Paul. DV prides itself on a unique selection of products for both you and your home. Each piece of locally made art, women's fashion, accessories, and gift items are hand-selected to ensure a high level of style and uniqueness, as well as a balance between quality and affordability.

Amanda Wilde

Q&A

What makes your business unique?
Clever displays and products change weekly. A new local artist is featured every month! Affordable prices redefine what it means to go "boutique shopping."

What would you like customers to know about your business?
Design Vertigo comes to you in three parts: retail, creative services and events. Enjoy everything Design Vertigo has to offer, including shopping, fashion shows, art classes and interior design for your home or business.

What is the best advice you've been given?
"When you think you're working hard, just work a little bit harder."
—Tracy Luther, as quoted by Del Howard

Edina Skin Care Specialists

7450 France Ave S, Ste 230, Edina, 952.920.5521
edinaskincare.com

Experienced. Innovative. Caring.
Edina Skin Care Specialists, located in the offices of MMK Plastic Surgery, is now 15 years old and boasts the most combined years of aesthetician expertise of any medical skin care practice in the Twin Cities. Built with a foundational focus on a customer's individual needs, Edina Skin Care Specialists is forward-thinking, keeping a finger on the pulse of industry developments in order to provide the best service possible.

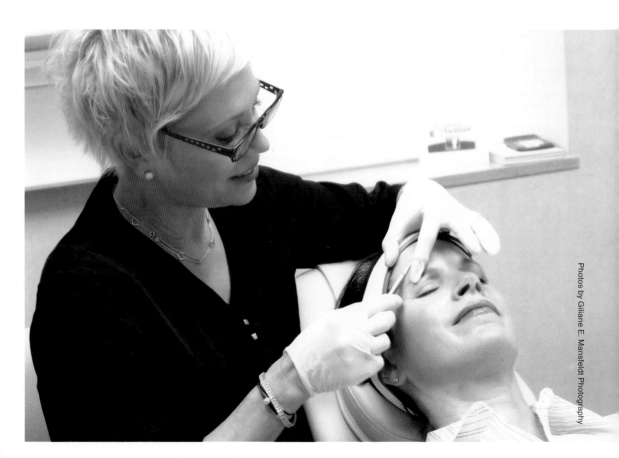

Photos by Giliane E. Mansfeldt Photography

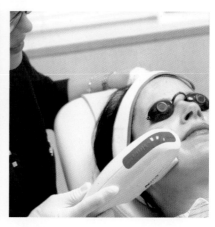

Cathleen Olson

⬛ Q&A

What would you like customers to
know about your business?
We are here to work with our customers
to achieve their most beautiful skin,
no matter their age or skin type.

What advice would you give women
who are starting a business?
Trust your instincts.

What is the biggest perk about
owning a small business?
I really enjoy the flexibility that owning
my own business affords. With our
size, we're very nimble, which allows
us to adapt to new trends quickly.

What is your biggest motivator?
Meeting a new client with an unresolved
skin issue and providing the care and
treatment necessary to turn them
into a happy, satisfied customer.

EuroNest

5700 W 36th St, Minneapolis, 952.929.2927
euro-nest.com, Twitter: @EuroNest

Authentic. Sustainable. Unique.
EuroNest is a premier boutique furniture retailer in the Twin Cities. Their talented interior designers create design plans for homes using one-of-a-kind European pieces, quality American-made reproduction furniture and gorgeous home accessories. EuroNest designs homes to be a unique reflection of the owners and how they live, as well as warm and comfortable.

Q&A

What would you like customers to know about your business?
Our European antiques are purchased mostly from France, Belgium and The Netherlands. The reproduction furniture includes lines such as Baker, Hickory Chair and Pearson. Our unique home accessories fill a niche in the home market.

Who is your role model or mentor?
I am smitten with the Queen of England!

What is your personal motto?
Be yourself, follow your dreams and passion, laugh a lot and enjoy every day—it is truly a gift. Always say, "Thank you."

What or who inspires you?
Inspiration comes from being creative, being smart at running a business and sticking to the core of the brand.

Lori Anderson

Leah Simon-Clarke

Q&A

What makes your business unique?
Our philosophy derives from knowing that when we make people feel beautiful, they act in beautiful ways. We set ego aside to strive for authentic beauty.

What is your favorite part of being an entrepreneur?
Living my dharma and enhancing people's lives by connecting with them and caring for others. I love learning about life through others' willingness to share their time and stories.

What is your personal motto?
Be honest with yourself and others. Take care of yourself, because the more you do, the more you can give. Play like a child as often as possible.

Extrados

4279 Sheridan Ave S, Minneapolis, 612.920.0051
extrados.com

Classic. Current. Purposeful.

Extrados has been providing superb service in the Twin Cities and surrounding areas for seven years. Extrados has cultivated a team who have an excellent ability to tap into your inner beauty. Extrados cares about getting to know what makes you shine. Their strong creative ability, ethics and dedication to caring about each individual is what allows you to walk out feeling your personal best.

Q&A

What makes your business unique?
Each client experience is tailored to
individual needs, expectations and
aspirations with an emphasis on service,
quality and enhancing natural beauty.

What would you like customers to know?
We see immense potential in everyone
and consistently promote each client
to new levels of confidence.

What advice would you give women
who are starting a business?
Be passionate, make a difference,
become irreplaceable and be yourself.

What is your personal motto?
Do more of what makes you happy.

Owner Sasha Westin with
Connie Schmidt and Lucille Pew

The Fabuliss Style Group

612.554.4629
fabuliss.com, Twitter: @fabuliss

Empowering. Effortless. Essential.
The Fabuliss Style Group is an image makeover team that specializes in personalized head-to-toe transformations. Packages, services and products enhance confidence for career changes, professional spotlight moments, seasonal updates, life milestones and special events. Fabuliss consistently exceeds client expectations with sessions ranging from private appointments to group events.

Farmer's Hat Productions

612.333.1610
burburandfriends.com, Twitter: @BurBursFriends

Empowering. Educational. Engaging.
Farmer's Hat Productions is committed to "Growing Kids Through Diverse Learning Experiences." Their unique Bur Bur & Friends line of award-winning children's books and products was designed to build kids' self esteem while teaching them about being active through sports and outdoor exploration. The company has also worked to create awareness about physical/health challenges that some children face, and to teach kids about real-life experiences.

JoAnne Pastel and Kakie Fitzsimmons

Q&A

What makes your business unique?
Farmer's Hat Productions was created to fill an unmet need for young children by providing resources that expose them to the diversity of the real world on many levels.

What would you like customers to know about your business?
It's more than a business... it's a passion. We are devoted to creating teachable moments for children, and building their self-esteem as they identify with and relate to our characters.

What is the best advice you've been given?
Follow your passion. Don't be afraid of rejection or of asking for help. Be persistent and have follow-through.

What or who inspires you?
Our characters are based on real-life children, including our own. As they learn, so do we! They teach us what really matters, which gives us the motivation to keep pressing forward.

What do you CRAVE?
For our efforts to make a difference in the lives of children and families.

Feather Blue Studios

651.489.8281
featherbluestudios.com

Model Integrity

modelintegrity.com

Modern. Vibrant. Captivating.
Shannon Tacheny of Feather Blue Studios specializes in modern portrait art, fashion photography and commercial projects, in-studio or on-location. Child and family photos are vibrant and expressive; high school senior sessions are fun, innovative, and fashion-forward. The studio's distinctive Model Integrity division focuses on helping aspiring models of all ages get started in the local talent industry.

Photos by Shannon Tacheny of Feather Blue Studios

Shannon Tacheny

Q&A

What makes your business unique?
My personal, artistic eye and my willingness to go above and beyond for my clients. Also the studio's collection of stylish patterned backgrounds that will make your neighbor (and your Christmas card list) jealous!

What would you like customers to know about your business?
Photography goes way beyond taking pictures. My job involves creative vision, intelligent in-the-moment decision-making and genuine client connections. I create modern art, lasting heirlooms and powerful icons.

What is your personal motto?
Life's perfect moments are now.

What do you CRAVE?
Chai tea. Dark chocolate. Authentic relationships.

Q&A

What is your favorite part of being an entrepreneur?
The most satisfying part of being an entrepreneur is developing and maintaining ongoing relationships with my customers.

What advice would you give women who are starting a business?
Running a business is similar to playing a competitive game; you can't win without good defense. You must constantly review expenses, so you don't get out-played and end up losing.

What is your personal motto?
When you don't want to do the registry... come to Fleurish!

Lindi Dillon

Photos by B Johnson Photos

Fleurish

701 E Lake St, Wayzata, 952.476.2296
fleurishllp.com

Exceptional. Charming. Local.
Fleurish began by creating custom holiday gift baskets for corporate clients.
In 2007, Fleurish opened a retail location in Wayzata and expanded their
product line to include personalized stationery, invitations, monogram gifts
and an extensive line of award-winning gourmet foods and tableware. Fleurish
strives to celebrate and passionately support local vendors. They have become
a premier shopping destination for specialty gifts for every occasion.

Photos by Stephanie Colgan Photography
except middle detail by Mimi Holliday

Flirt Boutique

177 Snelling Ave N, St Paul, 651.698.3692
flirt-boutique.com

Glamorous. Luxurious. Playful.
Flirt is a sexy-sweet lingerie boutique inspired by vintage Hollywood glamor and pin-up girls. With bras ranging in size from A to E, Flirt fills the niche for quality lingerie in the Twin Cities. Whether choosing everyday bras and panties or glamorous silk gowns, you'll feel fancier—and flirtier—which is the whole idea!

Jessica Gerard

Q&A

What would you like customers to know about your business?
Flirt has been a top five finalist the past two years for the national *Best of Intima* Award!

What is your favorite part of being an entrepreneur?
My "job" is not work. It's what I do for fun.

What is the biggest perk about owning a small business?
Flexibility.

Who is your role model or mentor?
Myself. I set my goals and I make them happen.

What is your personal motto?
If you are going to do something, you might as well take the time to do it right.

Lynn Gordon

Q&A

What makes your business unique?
Named by *Bon Appetit* as one of the best bread bakeries in the US, twice! We were the first organic bakery in the United States. Our outdoor 90-seat patio dining is in demand for breakfast, lunch *and* dinner from spring until late fall—pretty fabulous!

What would you like customers to know about your business?
Our mood! We are laid back, fun, unpretentious, confident, healthy and eco-minded. Our bartender Gretchin jazzes up the place with her exuberance for drink orders. Come check us out!

What can't you live without?
Our customers can't seem to live without our gluten-free options, coffee, Pretty in Pink Gluten-free Chocolate Layer Cake, Crab Cake Eggs Benedict, handmade pasta, Fish Tacos and seasonal and local ingredients.

French Meadow Bakery & Cafe

2610 Lyndale Ave S, Minneapolis, 612.870.7855
frenchmeadowcafe.com

Fresh. Eclectic. Organic.
Since 1984, French Meadow embodied everything that is real about food. They championed organic and promoted sustainable agriculture, fair trade and local farmers before it was popular. French Meadow makes and serves from-scratch, fresh food for breakfast, lunch and dinner. They grind Wild Acres turkey fresh daily for the popular Turkey Burger served on a 100 percent sprouted organic bun. Although "Best Vegetarian Restaurant" and the "PETA" Award are familiar honors for French Meadow, customers also adore their sustainably sourced, hormone-free bacon, bison, grass-fed beef, organic chicken, fresh wild-caught fish and lamb.

Photos by B Johnson Photos

Fusion LifeSpa

18142 Minnetonka Blvd, Deephaven, 952.345.3335
fusionlifespa.com

Authentic. Dynamic. Holistic.
Fusion LifeSpa provides health, beauty and rejuvenation in one inspired dwelling.
Part natural health clinic, part spa, they offer the finest in holistic beauty services
and time-honored health treatments from highly trained practitioners. The Fusion
Skin Care line represents the highest level of pure, results-oriented skin care
by combining the finest botanical ingredients and the latest technology.

Donna Duffy

Q&A

What makes your business unique?
Our combination of natural health care, holistic spa treatments and high-performance skin care services.

What would you like customers to know about your business?
Fusion LifeSpa was designed as an eco-friendly spa with low VOC paints and cork flooring. We source and create pure, result-oriented products that do not contain parabens or phthalates.

What is your personal motto?
One of our family values is "Dance like no one is watching." It is so important to be authentic—to be free to be your true self.

What do you CRAVE?
Uncluttered thoughts—free space.

Merry Beck

Q&A

What makes your business unique?
We are a retail-based gallery that works
with both emerging and mid-career
artistic talents under one roof, creating
a unique selection to the area.

What would you like customers to
know about your business?
Our tagline is "art in every degree,"
which is fitting for an environment that
celebrates all art forms and strives
to stay cutting-edge and original.

What can't you simply live
without in your business?
Jewelry, jewelry, jewelry! We work with
some of the country's most talented
jewelry artists, both local and national.

Gallery 360

3011 W 50th St, Minneapolis, 612.925.2400
gallery360mpls.com

Original. Local. Artisan.
Gallery 360 is a female-owned and operated gallery in the southwest area
of Minneapolis, featuring a unique selection of fine art, jewelry, clothing and
handmade goods. This passionate crew of women work to recreate the gallery
every six weeks to offer the finest selection of local and national talents.

Photos by Louisa Podlich

Vasilia Pasalis Sedgwick

Q&A

What makes your business unique?
Having the ability to assess and quickly
identify the needs and wants of my
clients after the initial consultation.

What would you like customers to
know about your business?
The end result saves my clients time,
money and creates true peace of mind.

What is your favorite part of
being an entrepreneur?
The reward of working with a diverse
clientele and watching their habits evolve
into healthier lifestyles. I have the ability
to share what I know with others.

What is the best advice you've been given?
Don't limit yourself.

Who is your role model or mentor?
My grandmothers. They were women
of strength, grace and courage.

What is your personal motto?
When your personal spaces are pulled
together, you have more control and
clarity in your life. Less is more.

Get Organized Inc.

507.319.8874
getorganizedmn.com

Practical. Efficient. Trusted.
Get Organized Inc. collaborates with the client to create personalized organizational systems according to what fits their busy lifestyle. Professional Organizer Vasilia Sedgwick transforms residential and small business environments into well-functioning spaces with a flair of aesthetic appeal.

Gianni's Steakhouse

635 Lake St E, Wayzata, 952.404.1100
giannis-steakhouse.com

Mouthwatering. Delectable. Scrumptious.
Gianni's serves prime steaks and fresh seafood in a casual setting on Lake
Minnetonka. Gianni's provides the perfect vibrant atmosphere to enjoy a cocktail
or choose a drink from an extensive list of imported and domestic wines. Enjoy
their beautiful outdoor patio seating during Minnesota's gorgeous spring, summer
and early fall. Boaters have loved Gianni's extensive Dockside To Go menu
for years as a fabulous way to enjoy an elegant meal while on the lake!

Terri Huml

Q&A

What makes your business unique?
Our great selection of prime beef and fresh seafood, impeccable service and an energetic atmosphere from lunch through late-night dinners. I take great pride in ensuring my guests have a wonderful experience when dining with us.

What is your favorite part of being an entrepreneur?
Controlling your own destiny. You reap the rewards of hard work. Nothing makes me happier than hearing my lunch and dinner guests tell me how much they enjoyed their meal.

What is your biggest motivator?
My business is an extension of my home, I love hosting friends and I get to do it everyday—and I don't have to cook and wash the dishes.

Giliane E. Mansfeldt

Q&A

What makes your business unique?
My business is a photography
business run by a woman, for women.
I have a coop gallery/studio that is
available for shoots as well.

What is the best advice you've been given?
If you can dream it, you can achieve it. All
you have to do is follow your dreams.

Who is your role model or mentor?
My role model is my mother. If it was
not for her, I would not be where I am
today. I have much to thank her for.

What is your personal motto?
Stand up for what you believe in,
even if it means standing alone.

What do you CRAVE?
Happiness, laughing as much as
possible and, above all else, love.

Giliane E. Mansfeldt Photography

612.387.6181
giliane-e-mansfeldtphotography.com, Twitter: @GEMPhoto326

Creative. Innovative. Respectful.
Giliane E. Mansfeldt's goal is to inspire change and challenge social norms using only her camera. While classically trained in fine art photography, Giliane felt there was an under-representation of photographers supporting women and women-owned businesses. Giliane has dedicated her skills to supporting women clients and women-owned businesses, charities, nonprofits and clubs.

GirlmeetsGeek

361.433.5388
girlmeetsgeek.com, Twitter: @girlmeetsgeek

Engaging. Intelligent. Heartfelt.
Kate-Madonna Hindes is an industry leader, national trainer and author on emotional integrity and authenticity in today's handheld and online media. Notably, she sits on the coaching panel for Keith Ferrazzi's Relationship Academy alongside Chris Brogan and Tony Hsieh. Either in an auditorium setting or one-on-one, Kate-Madonna excels at simplifying mobile advertising and social media in a way companies truly understand.

Main photo courtesy of GirlMeetsGeek, additional photos by Giliane E. Mansfeldt Photography

Q&A

What makes your business unique?
GirlmeetsGeek is all about passion. I analyze, define, tweak and ultimately help you succeed online with your most passionate and authentic self.

What can't you simply live without in your business?
I'm currently in a very successful relationship with my smartphone. I love the functionality and being able to communicate without missing a beat.

What is the best advice you've been given?
Someone once told me, "Be Teflon." By allowing nothing to stick to us and leave a mark, we cultivate knowledge from our experiences without bitterness.

What is the biggest perk about owning a small business?
I have the privilege of standing in front of Fortune 100 CEOs and those I once only read about. It's an incredible honor.

What is your personal motto?
I have a Rule of Three for social media: be authentic, be original and bring those online connections offline—that's where the true magic happens.

Kate-Madonna Hindes

Greenbody Greenplanet

888.201.8608
greenbodygreenplanet.com, Twitter: @gbgplanet

Hairs to You Salon

651.628.0286
hairs2yousalon.com, Twitter: @hairs2you

Eco-active. Conscious. Beautiful.
Greenbody Greenplanet is the hair care line you've been searching for! Just ask the customers at their flagship salon, Hairs to You. They offer zero-toxin, low-environmental impact, 100 percent certified organic plant-based ingredients that are deeply nourishing, color-protecting and safe for you. The rich, creamy lather and soothing aroma is sure to impress, and the results will captivate you, leaving you to wonder how you ever showered without it!

Q&A

What makes your business unique?
We are more than just hair care. We inspire a lifestyle choice for women and men everywhere who seek to be beautiful—inside and out.

What would you like customers to know about your business?
I am a local salon owner, hairstylist, and wife of a two-time cancer survivor. When I couldn't find "clean" products that delivered the results I was accustomed to, I created them!

What advice would you give women who are starting a business?
Enjoy the journey. The final destination is fluid and will change as you change. Be willing to adapt and roll with whatever challenges arise. And have fun!

Lorri Weisen

Happy Couple Company

612.840.3501
happycouplecompany.com

Wise. Inspiring. Happy.
Need the perfect but non-registry wedding or shower gift? Know a newly engaged couple? Want to acknowledge the magical, mundane qualities of your own partner? Happy Couple Company is your source for the hippest, smartest gifts to celebrate relationships. Created by Dr. Carol Bruess, co-author of the nationally recognized and award-winning book, "What Happy Couples Do," the Happy Couple Company is your source for the coolest couple gifts ever.

Carol Bruess, Ph.D

Q&A

What makes your business unique?
No doubt, the expertise. Happy Couple gifts are not only beautiful, they are wise. They are not only witty, but inspiring. They are not only fun, they're educational (but without the homework).

What would you like customers to know about your business?
As a relationships expert, I've been featured on Oprah Radio, the national CBS "Early Morning Show," in *Cosmo* magazine (often!), and given multiple dozens of media interviews.

What can't you simply live without in your business?
A husband with a great sense of humor (and a really cool commitment to our 25 years of happy-coupledom).

Q&A

What makes your business unique?
We expose our staff to creativity and growth, which makes them excited to do amazing hair! We sponsor photo shoots, host art shows and are active in fashion.

What would you like customers to know about your business?
At HAUS we *are* hair, keeping your look up-to-date, yet completely "you." Our clients are age 9 to 99. What they all have in common is a tendency toward being fabulous.

What is the best advice you've been given?
Don't be afraid to work hard! Never ask your team to do something you wouldn't do yourself. Lead by example and earn the respect of your team.

Jessica Reipke

HAUS Salon

4240 Nicollet Ave, Minneapolis, 612.827.4287
haussalon.com

Modern. Bold. Beautiful.
The stylists of HAUS Salon have created a vibe that is high-energy, chic and modern—you'll feel like you're in New York or LA, instead of nestled in convenient south Minneapolis. Their focus on technique is intense, but their personalities aren't. Influenced by the Bauhaus movement, this spacious salon showcases local artists and treats guests to before and after photos of their new style.

Hazel & Haverly

hazelandhaverly.com, Twitter: @hazelandhaverly

attagirl by kedrin

attagirlbykedrin.com, Twitter: @attagirlcrochet

Handmade. Creative. Fashion-forward.
Hazel & Haverly and attagirl by kedrin offer high-quality, handmade fashion accessories for discerning women who appreciate unique pieces. For attagirl by kedrin, Kedrin Likness designs and handcrafts affordable on-trend accessories for every season. Her high-fashion line, Hazel & Haverly, offers one-of-a-kind, custom-made treasures with the finest of yarns.

Q&A

What makes your business unique?
I take the vintage craft of crochet and bring it into the 21st century by using on-trend colors and styling. My fashion-forward, modern pieces are a delight to wear.

What would you like customers to know about your business?
Our goal is to provide our customers with high-fashion clothing and accessories that are handmade locally.

What advice would you give women who are starting a business?
Often an outsider's perspective is the most eye-opening one.

What is your biggest motivator?
I'm motivated by the challenges of staying creative and relevant. I strive to make each collection better than the last.

Kedrin Likness

What is your personal motto?

"*Play like a child as often as possible.*"

Leah Simon-Clarke of Extrados

Landmark Plaza by Elijah Parker

Q&A

What makes your business unique?
I can coach anyone, anywhere via the miracle of distance (phone or Skype) coaching. Many of my clients aren't even in my time zone!

What would you like customers to know about your business?
My individual coaching program is not one-size-fits-all. Everyone has unique bio-individuality and symptoms. I am each of my clients' champion—their personal advocate in their quest for optimal health.

What can't you simply live without in your business?
The immense reward and satisfaction of seeing my clients' health transform during our work together. Their milestones are my milestones; their successes are my successes.

What is your favorite part of being an entrepreneur?
I love the creative thinking process that doesn't require approval from others. I am free to make my own choices and create new products on my own terms.

What is your personal motto?
Don't let the perfect be the enemy of the good.

Jill Grunewald

Healthful Elements LLC

612.840.2034
healthfulelements.com, Twitter: @JGrunewaldHNC

Informed. Educational. Transformative.
Healthful Elements is a holistic nutrition and health program focusing on teaching women with hypothyroidism and adrenal fatigue how to nourish their bodies with whole foods and lifestyle choices that create balance. This allows them to regain energy, shed weight and alleviate other symptoms while still enjoying foods they love. Jill is also a health and wellness writer for several popular publications.

Photos by Shannon Tacheny of Feather Blue Studios

Health Foundations Family Health & Birth Center

968 Grand Ave, St Paul, 651.895.2520
health-foundations.com

Innovative. Family-centered. Welcoming.
Health Foundations is a free-standing birth center where clients receive personal
attention and extraordinary care in an intimate family-centered, home-like setting.
New moms build relationships with Health Foundations midwives and staff and
receive individualized support during this miraculous and transformative event. Health
Foundations has created a warm, safe, loving environment, with birth suites that
are spacious, beautifully decorated and provide luxurious tubs for water births.

Dr. Amy Johnson-Grass

Q&A

What would you like customers to know about your business?
We have a lactation center, support groups and well women clinic. We also offer yoga and various educational classes. We have a naturopathic pediatric and fertility practice at the Center.

What is your favorite part of being an entrepreneur?
Being an entrepreneur gives me opportunities to meet wonderful people who are so inspiring. I love being part of the local community and networking with other business owners.

What is the biggest perk about owning a small business?
It's nice to be the decision maker and be able to implement my vision of providing a patient-centered, holistic model of care driven by the needs of the families we help.

Q&A

What makes your business unique?
This homegrown business is results
oriented. With 25 years of experience,
a loyal following and trusted reputation,
Heaven On Earth offers the ultimate healing
and therapeutic massage experience.

What would you like customers to
know about your business?
The massage session is all inclusive.
Aroma and stone therapy are integrated
into every massage. Knowledge in many
techniques round off the intuitive and holistic
experience. No massage is ever the same.

What advice would you give women
who are starting a business?
Love what you do; make it your own and put
your own character and authenticity into it.

What is the biggest perk about
owning a small business?
When you have the opportunity
to inject your own vitality into the
business and experience success,
it's like Heaven on Earth!

What or who inspires you?
Those who have, against all odds
or hardships, grown and become
purposeful and compassionate and
then share that with their world.

Jean McCoy Koury

Heaven On Earth Therapeutic Massage

5009 Excelsior Blvd, Ste 144, St Louis Park, 952.926.3928

Genuine. Nurturing. Experienced.
Heaven On Earth is an oasis for the mind, body and spirit. Upon arriving, restful music eases the mind and calming aromas comfort the spirit, preparing the body for a soothing, transforming massage. Highly skilled hands nurture the muscles, providing essential tension relief for ultimate relaxation and wellness.

Photos by Gillane E. Mansfeldt Photography

Photos by B Johnson Photos

Hollywood Fashion Secrets

612.548.5000
hollywoodfashionsecrets.com, Twitter: @Hollywood_FS

Innovative. Experts. Global.
Hollywood Fashion Secrets (HFS) performs undercover wardrobe magic for women everywhere. Fashion fairy godmothers Marni and Jane are dedicated to preventing wardrobe malfunctions across the country. Hollywood Fashion Tape, the product that started it all, was inspired by a hapless gaping sweater in need of closure. Now, every clever, problem-solving HFS product is designed to help women feel confident and look their best everywhere, every time.

Q&A

What makes your business unique?
HFS was the first company to manufacture and market unique fashion solution products, and received the *Allure* "Best of Beauty" award for creating the new category called Fashion First Aid.

What would you like customers to know about your business?
We are part Hollywood stylist, part savvy girlfriend—the one who has your back (and front) and everything else you need to be perfectly put together!

What advice would you give women who are starting a business?
Proceed without fear. You don't need all the answers, just a curiosity. Stick to it and believe in yourself! Malcolm Gladwell claims it takes 10,000 hours to become an expert.

Jane Dailey and Marni Bumsted

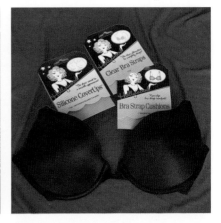

Amber Toste

Q&A

What makes your business unique?
We hold the exclusive rights to many brands, pride ourselves on offering superior customer service, carry a mix of price ranges and 100 percent of our denim is made in the USA.

What can't you simply live without in your business?
Dedicated and fashionable customers, amazing employees and Diet Coke!

What is your favorite part of being an entrepreneur?
Knowing that when women walk through the door they will experience an escape from their otherwise demanding and stressful lives and leave with amazing items.

What is your personal motto?
The size on the tag doesn't matter—how it fits does!

Houndstooth

5749 Egan Dr, Savage, 952.440.2807
582 Prairie Center Dr, #223, Eden Prairie, 952.261.2974
houndstoothboutique.com, Twitter: @houndstoothmn

Fashion-forward. Service-driven. Quality.
Houndstooth is a boutique like no other. Owner Amber Toste has an exceptional knowledge of fashion that goes beyond most; she specializes in pairing unusual finds with traditional pieces to fuse together a personal style, leaving the customer asking for more. Houndstooth also carries one-of-a-kind jewelry, premium clothing, denim and handmade shoes from all over the world. You won't be disappointed.

Kristi Berkvam Stratton

Q&A

What would you like customers to
know about your business?
A fantastic style shop with only good,
fairly priced "junk" that is guaranteed
to put a smile on your face. Come
find your prize at hunt & gather.

What is your favorite part of
being an entrepreneur?
I believe in the rough individualism
of the true American spirit. I have
always felt confident plotting my own
course. I delight in taking risks.

What is the best advice you've been given?
Practice admiration, not envy. Always
learn from others. Stay true to yourself, be
original, have ideas and have an identity that
is truly yours—not a diluted copycat version.

hunt & gather

4944 Xerxes Ave S, Minneapolis, 612.455.0250
huntandgatherantiques.com

Kooky. Fresh. Unusual.
Expect the unexpected at hunt & gather. Discover goodies that are curious,
odd and funky. This shop is ever-changing and fully stocked with fun, hip found
objects jammed into two levels by 20 aggressively "hunting" dealers. You'll find
a fantastic selection of taxidermy, oil paintings, giant letters, flashcards, Sandy
Stone upholstered pieces, Tommy Brandt Designs, furniture and architectural
elements, advertising and more! New stock bought and sold daily.

Photos by Gillane E. Mansfeldt Photography

il Vostro Boutique

5045 France Ave S, Edina, 612.920.3167
ilvostroboutique.com

Classic. Delightful. Enchanting.
il Vostro Boutique searches for under-the-radar designers from abroad as well
as local ones to offer customers stylish, special pieces that aren't available
elsewhere in the Twin Cities. Owner Katie Egan brings her Manhattan fashion
industry experience to her 50th & France shopping haven. il Vostro Boutique
strives to appeal to women of a variety of ages and lifestyles and carries both
trend-driven and classic pieces in a charming, friendly environment.

Photos by Shannon Tacheny of FeatherBlue Studios

Katie Egan

Q&A

What makes your business unique?
il Vostro Boutique offers a warm, welcoming
environment with unique pieces from around
the world as well as locally-made items.
The majority of items are under $300.

What can't you simply live
without in your business?
The support of my friends and family. Most
of my friends and family have worked
in the shop, including my grandma.

What is your biggest motivator?
My love for fashion and the industry. After
working in Manhattan in various roles within
the industry, I still just can't get enough!

What or who inspires you?
The excitement of discovering a
new, up-and-coming designer and
seeing the new collections they
develop season after season.

Ashley Robinson (standing),
Rhonda Robinson and BJ Hall

Q&A

What makes your business unique?
Our personalized service! We really live our
motto: We Bring The World To Your Door.

What would you like customers to
know about your business?
We love working with people who
want to build lifelong relationships and
friendships. We want to help make every
trip unique and special, because your
time and memories are valuable.

What can't you simply live
without in your business?
Great relationships with clients and
suppliers, the ability to think quickly,
my laptop and a little caffeine!

What do you CRAVE?
To never look back and say, "I wish I
would have..." "To live each day and
savor it for what it is—a (the) present."

Indigo Journeys LLC

763.498.7754
indigojourneys.com

Personalized. Empowering. Passionate.
Indigo Journeys is a full-service travel consultancy firm that caters to the needs of the insightful traveler. Combining first-hand destination knowledge, strong industry contacts and a true desire to know you, they craft unforgettable experiences for clients. They will support and inspire you to experience the world the way you have always dreamed of. Let Indigo Journeys bring the world to your door!

Main photo and protrait by B Johnson Photos, additional photos by Claude Dagenais and gerenme.

Infrared Studio

612.269.1662
infraredstudio.com, Twitter: @infraredstudio

Edgy. Engaging. Exceptional.
Infrared Studio, an atelier owned by interdisciplinary artist Lauren Nicole, embodies an aesthetic that speaks to everyone from riot grrrls (of all ages!) to more mature women who don't take their style cues from mainstream media's fashion police. The pieces here are ahead-of-trend—edgy, elegant and unconventional.

 # Q&A

What makes your business unique?
In a word: me. I bring my personal
aesthetic to bear on everything I do,
whether I'm creating a jewelry collection,
a new product, brand or a website.

What would you like customers to
know about your business?
I'm a bit of a Renaissance woman; my
background spans fine art, design,
photography, marketing, and interactive
media. Have an interesting design
project you need help with? Let's talk!

What can't you simply live
without in your business?
Fashionistas and visionaries. Women
who are always on the lookout for cutting-
edge ideas and cool new products.

Lauren Nicole Rusnak

Jennifer Merchant Design

612.710.4595
jennifermerchantdesign.com, Twitter: @JenMDesign

Innovative. Bold. Fashion-forward.
Jewelry unlike any other, Jennifer Merchant Design offers wearable art for the fashion conscious. This high-quality, handcrafted label—created by Minneapolis designer Jennifer Merchant—blurs the line between art and fashion. Combining materials and techniques that are both traditional and experimental, Jennifer's jewelry is as intriguing as it is beautiful. Bold and fashion-forward, this is jewelry that gets you noticed!

Main photo by Robb Long courtesy of *l'etoile Magazine*, additional photos by Jacqueline Smith of Juniper Seahorses

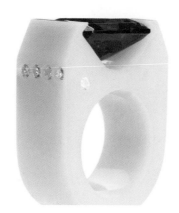

Jennifer Merchant

Q&A

What makes your business unique?
I make jewelry using a technique I invented to layer acrylic with found imagery. I also create designs that incorporate the solid surface material Corian with fine metals and gems.

What would you like customers to know about your business?
I specialize in one-of-a-kind and custom-order creations. You can find my work for sale online as well as in local boutiques and galleries such as Bumbershute and Gallery 360.

What is your favorite part of being an entrepreneur?
Creative problem solving. So much goes into running a business, especially when you also design the product, that there is never a shortage of things to learn and problems to solve.

Judith McGrann & Friends, Inc.

4615 Excelsior Blvd, Minneapolis, 612.922.2971
judithmcgrannandfriends.com

Fresh. Fun. Friendly.
This mother-daughter boutique has been a vibrant, uplifting and welcoming Twin Cities destination for nearly three decades. They specialize in high-quality, easy-to-wear clothing and an ever-changing mix of jewelry, accessories and one-of-a-kind finds. Customers rave about the service, the comfortable environment and the joy in knowing they'll leave with a look that's truly their own.

Q&A

What makes you unique?
Our great staff specializes in helping you put
"your look" together—for as long as it takes.

What would you like customers to know?
We always tuck a good thought into
every package that leaves our store.

What do you CRAVE? In business? In life?
Our passion is helping each
customer look and feel her best.

WHAT do you CRAVE?
We love finding small chef-owned
restaurants in any city we visit.

Judith McGrann & Meghan McGrann

Jackie Just

Q&A

What would you like customers to
know about your business?
I don't consider myself the floral vendor,
but part of the event design team. I'm
passionate about we do here and always
strive for floral that is unique and mindful.

What can't you simply live
without in your business?
Handwritten notes. With so much
technology these days, a handwritten
thank you note goes a long way.

Who is your role model or mentor?
Women who have mastered the
balance of business ownership,
relationships and motherhood.

What is your biggest motivator?
Making each wedding or event more
unique and personal than the next.

Just Bloomed

5255 Chicago Ave S, Minneapolis, 612.600.9033
just-bloomed.com, Twitter: @JustBloomed

Lush. Vibrant. Stylish.
Just Bloomed is an award-winning fresh floral design studio specializing
in weddings and events. Owner Jackie Just is sought after for her artistic
talent in bringing a client's vision to life, signature clutter-free look, and
smart designs that have captured the attention of Twin Cities brides, local
and national publications, and TV shows as well as landed her the honor
of being named *Minnesota Bride* magazine's Best Florist of 2011.

Photos by Sewell Photography

Kara Jensen Zitnick, Esq. and Tracy Corcoran

Q&A

What makes your business unique?
LaunchHER is your one-stop source for all things entrepreneurs need—business AND legal—by providing brands with legal protection and business-savvy advice.

What is your favorite part of being an entrepreneur?
We love being a champion of women-owned brands. It is so exciting to watch a brand flourish under LaunchHER's expert guidance.

What advice would you give women who are starting a business?
Hire us. Starting a business out on the right foot is money well-spent.

What is your biggest motivator?
Witnessing our clients' daily successes.

What is your personal motto?
Tracy: Eat dessert first.
Kara: When in doubt, buy the shoes.

What or who inspires you?
Coffee. Desserts. Red nail polish. Stylish stationery. Creating a legacy.

LaunchHER

612.275.6317
launchher.com, Twitter: @LaunchHER, @LaunchHERLaw

Entrepreneurial. Distinctive. Connected.
LaunchHER gives a boost to women-owned brands by providing flat-fee business and legal services to companies at all stages. Their marketing, social media and brand development consultations grow brands beyond expectations. Flat-fee legal services protect brands through affordable trademark, copyright, business formation and individualized contracts.

Q&A

What would you like customers to
know about your business?
Bring a project and join us in the knitting
room, knit or shop to your heart's delight.

What can't you simply live
without in your business?
We are a supportive, inspiring yarn and
gift shop. We help any customer with
their fiber project with great conversation.
And the gifts are remarkable.

What advice would you give women
who are starting a business?
Go big. Create the wow factor and treat
your customers as the most special
people in the world. And be honest.

What is the best advice you've been given?
To go big or go home.

Polly Hart and Kirsten Skoglund

Lila and Claudine's Yarn & Gifts

86 Mahtomedi Ave, Mahtomedi, 651.429.9551
lilaandclaudines.com, Twitter: @lilaandclaudine

Exciting. Unique Supportive.
Entering Lila and Claudine's is like "going down the rabbit hole" or "jumping through the looking glass." The kaleidoscope of color around the room fills you with excited inspiration. You see fiber full of color and texture; there are creative ideas around every corner. A clever collection of gifts peeks out of nooks and crannies, giving you a host of ideas for the perfect present or prize!

Lisa Rubin Wardrobe Consulting LLC

612.747.6695
wardrobeconsulting.net

Sophisticated. Efficient. Impeccable.
Long considered a secret weapon among the most savvy businesswomen, Lisa Rubin provides exceptional service to men and women of all professions and incomes. For more than 25 years, Lisa's discriminating style has commanded a level of sophistication for her clientele that has no equal in the Twin Cities. With impeccable taste and confidence, Lisa offers such an incredibly effective service within every woman's budget and lifestyle that her clients return season after season, year after year.

Main photo by studioTart additional
photos by Darin Back Photography

Lisa Rubin

Q&A

What makes your business unique?
I give my clients assurance that they will be able to confidently go about their day and never worry about what they look like again. Regardless of their size, budget or profession, my clients are always dressed for success.

What would you like customers to know about your business?
My clients actually spend less on clothes because every piece works. I work fast and smart—my clients are very busy and I save them hours and hours by styling them efficiently and effectively.

What is your favorite part of being an entrepreneur?
Using what I was always told was a "special gift." I get to work every day with smart women and men of all professions as a their fashion guru, coach and therapist!

Local D'Lish

208 N First St, Minneapolis, 612.886.3047
localdlish.com

Local. Fresh. Organic.
Local D'Lish is a delightful cross between your neighborhood grocery store
and a farmer's market. They focus on high-quality, small-batch products
from local farmers/food artisans. Every product has a story that the staff
at Local D'Lish is eager to share with their customers. This "reconnection"
with food has created a bit of magic right here in this little store.

ⅷ Q&A

What would you like customers to know about your business?
We host a variety of fun events: cooking classes, food tours, fundraisers, etc. Our most popular event is our indoor winter market, which is held the third Saturday of every month from November–April, 10 a.m.–2 p.m.

What advice would you give women who are starting a business?
Remember to balance your life. Take time for all the things that make you who you are—family, friends, music, art—whatever it is, don't neglect it just to build your business.

What or who inspires you?
All of the small farmers and food artisans who put their heart and soul into creating wonderful food.

Ann Yin

Heather Bray and Jodi Ayres

Q&A

What makes your business unique?
The Lowbrow is the only spot in south Minneapolis where unpretentious bar food meets farm fresh ingredients! The funky decor is the brain child of mega-cool design team Aesthetic Apparatus.

What would you like customers to know about your business?
Weekend brunch is our best-kept secret. Fluffy from-scratch raspberry pancakes go great with blueberry mimosas and the spicy Jalapeno Hash is perfect with our house Sake Bloody Mary.

What is your favorite part of being an entrepreneur?
Getting the opportunity to create a community where kindness and respect are of the highest priority is so satisfying. We respect each other, our guests and the earth.

The Lowbrow

4244 Nicollet Ave S, Minneapolis, 612.208.0720
thelowbrowmpls.com, Twitter: @TheLowbrowMpls

Hip. Organic. Delicious.
The Lowbrow is a new restaurant that brings highbrow ingredients into a lowbrow
scene. The Lowbrow offers all your tavern favorites with a from-scratch, local twist.
Think burgers made with grass-fed Stone Bridge beef, hand-cut fries, from-scratch
nachos, and hand-stuffed jalapeno poppers. A great list of regional beers and
thoughtfully chosen wines make this the newest south Minneapolis destination.

Take home a prepared dinner for an easy meal tonight!

Lucia's Restaurant, Wine Bar and To Go

1432 W 31st St, Minneapolis, 612.825.1572
lucias.com

Delicious. Inviting. Real.
Lucia's is a Minneapolis landmark! Using the highest quality ingredients, Lucia's Restaurant, Wine Bar and Lucia's To Go offer something for everyone, including melt-in-your-mouth muffins, pastries and breads. Lucia's creates a weekly changing menu serving lunch and dinner for dining in or to go, along with a full bar offering organic wines and delicious cocktails. Enjoy all this and more in an intimate, warm and inviting environment.

Lucia Watson

Q&A

What makes your business unique?
The fresh food that actually tastes so, so good and our friendly, informed servers who really care about your experience.

What would you like customers to know about your business?
We have a full liquor license for our restaurant, wine bar and Lucia's To Go, and offer easy parking. We own the parking lot next door and have a $5 valet year round in the evenings.

What can't you simply live without in your business?
The fresh food!

What advice would you give women who are starting a business?
Find a good mentor, be passionately determined, and watch your nickels and dimes.

Erica Cooper and Alicia Danzig

Q&A

What makes your business unique?
Our collaborative approach to design allows the designer, artist and client to come together to create amazing spaces. We start with functional beauty and work to make each home reflect the client's lifestyle, taste, and needs.

What is your favorite part of being an entrepreneur?
Our *amazing* clients! We are both so blessed to serve the very best clientele, in not only the Twin Cities, but throughout the US and internationally.

What do you CRAVE?
Dark chocolate; celebrating the little moments; and uninspired walls, floors, ceilings and homes that beg for our creative inspiration and hands.

Lulu & Lilly's

314 W 38th St, Minneapolis, 763.441.6950, 612.275.6744
luluandlillys.com, lulupainting.com, yourstyleredesigned.com, Twitter: @ColorGypsy

Inspired. Unique. Personalized.
Lulu & Lilly's is a collaboration of two businesses that focuses on artisan painting
and interior design. It's a color and design playhouse for creative partners
Alicia Danzig of LULU Painting and Erica Cooper of Your Style reDesigned.
The shop is equal parts design space and boutique shopping. In addition, they
house creative workshops galore. Homeowners who long for the resources
to pull together a uniquely personalized home will need to look no further.

Lynne Garon Personal Training and Pilates, LLC

612.242.1642
lynnegaron.com

Compassionate. Progressive. Educational.
For more than 25 years, Lynne Garon has been working hard to keep her clients fit, strong and healthy. Her impressive array of clients range from busy corporate executives to patients recovering from injuries to fashionable women. Her approach is caring, but effective. She combines her numerous certifications, including strength training, Pilates and yoga to create a highly-customized program for each unique client.

Lynne Garon

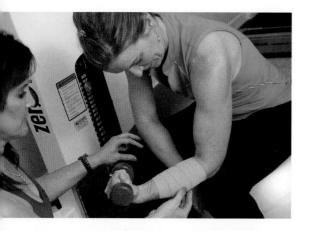

Q&A

What makes your business unique?
A self-described "education junkie," Lynne continually seeks certification training—and as a result is trusted by the many orthopedic surgeons and physical therapists who refer their patients to her care.

What can't you simply live without in your business?
My Cadillac Table, aka: "Lynne's Miracle Table." As we age, our muscles tighten and postures change. I can work wonders for my clients within a short time on this table.

What advice would you give women who are starting a business?
Educate, educate, educate. Become an expert in your field and never stop learning. Learn from the best and you will be the best. Teach with love, care and excellence.

Who is your role model or mentor?
My mother, who always told me a women should be strong, independent and able to stand on her own two feet. She was a woman truly ahead of her time.

What is your personal motto?
Life is not a "dress rehearsal." It's the final play. Make the most of every single day.

What do you CRAVE?
Excellent health, inner strength and love.

Krista Fragola

Q&A

What makes your business unique?
We are dedicated to supporting the
community through our Maha Movement.
We put the spotlight on our amazing
customers each month and raise awareness
for the charities that inspire them.

What would you like customers to
know about your business?
maha! strives to push boundaries and break
the rules. It is a place that encourages
women to evolve their style based on
inspiration. It is much more than activewear.

What do you CRAVE?
Vacations! I love my job, but
it's always healthy to get away,
rejuvenate and find clarity.

maha!

631 Lake St E, Wayzata, 952.873.7001
mahaactivewear.com, Twitter: @maha_activewear

Current. Bold. Inspired.
maha! is a destination where women who love fashion will be inspired by a unique selection, coveted designers, and an exciting philosophy of mixing special pieces together in unexpected ways for the modern active lifestyle. maha! is highly regarded for their carefully edited blend of apparel, accessories and jewelry for those not afraid to mix fashion with everyday life.

Kathleen A. Marron, JD, ACC

Q&A

What makes your business unique?
Our holistic approach. Executive coaches empower. Leadership consultants enlighten. Speakers inspire. We do all three, connecting your strengths and passions to results, paving your unique path to success.

What can't you simply live without in your business?
A sense of humor; an organizationally gifted executive assistant and creative variety.

What is your favorite part of being an entrepreneur?
The freedom to be creative, take risks, and explore people's stories. Each day is a new adventure. I love bringing people hope and helping them achieve their dreams!

What advice would you give women who are starting a business?
Be curious, creative and courageous. Know your strengths (and blind spots). Kill the ANTs (automatic negative thoughts) through renewing your mind. Finally, get good financial advice (and your own success coach).

Who inspires you?
Among mere mortals I'd include: Eleanor Roosevelt, Peter Drucker, Amelia Earhart, Katherine Hepburn, Maya Angelou, and my incredibly gifted clients, family and friends.

The Marron Alliance, LLC

612.751.4444
marronalliance.com

Inspiring. Insightful. Transformative.
Kathleen Marron provides a portfolio of professional services to help individuals
and teams achieve success. Her clients rave about her keen ability to tailor her
services to their needs: turning thoughts into action, deriving clarity from chaos,
and equipping them for sustainable change as they achieve their ideal future.

Max's

Shops at Excelsior & Grand; 3826 Grand Way, St Louis Park, 952.922.8364
stylebymax.com, Twitter: @stylebymax

Cool. Urban. Artistic.

Chic and casual, Max's has built a reputation as a jewelry store unlike any other
in the Twin Cities. Max's features artist-designed-and-made fine jewelry, home
décor and specialty chocolates from around the world. In 2011, Max's was
named the Coolest Small Store in America by *INSTORE* magazine. Discover
this unique collection at The Shops at Excelsior & Grand in St. Louis Park.

Ellen Hertz

 Q&A

What would you like customers to know about your business?
We host approximately 10 jewelry designer trunk shows each year, giving our customers an insiders' opportunity to meet the personalities behind their jewelry purchases.

What is your favorite part of being an entrepreneur?
Having the freedom to determine when the time is right to try new ideas— products, strategies, promotions— without interference from anyone.

What is your biggest motivator?
Loyal, repeat customers!

What do you CRAVE?
Jewelry and chocolate, of course!

Samantha J. Strong

Q&A

What makes your business unique?
As a woman-owned construction company, Metamorphosis is rare enough. When you include the real estate brokerage and green sensibility, we truly become one of a kind.

What can't you simply live
without in your business?
As I am working in two industries with poor reputations, the answer is simple: integrity, honesty and communication.

What is the best advice you've been given?
"Leap and the net will appear."
—John Burroughs

Who is your role model or mentor?
To those who have mentored me over the years, thank you. But some things you can't learn. I'd like to think that I inherited spirit and drive from my grandma.

What or who inspires you?
My team. When I was working solo, although the work was rewarding, there was no support. Now my team and I all work together, doing more collectively than any one of us could do alone.

Metamorphosis

612.782.2000
morphmpls.com, Twitter: @MorphMpls

Sustainable. Vibrant. Knowledgeable.
Metamorphosis is trailblazing a new path in Twin Cities housing. Integrating
real estate and construction, they're experts in their fields and bring a
sense of environmental stewardship to each client experience. Growing
more than 300 percent last year, Metamorphosis is on the way up! Now is
the time to buy, sell, or renovate your home or business. You can expect
Metamorphosis to provide unsurpassed service, value and results.

State Fair by B Johnson Photos

What is your favorite part of
being an entrepreneur?

" New ideas make me feel
like I've just injected a pint
of espresso in my arm. "

Carol Bruess, PhD, of Happy Couple Company

Melissa Miroslavich

Q&A

What makes your business unique?
We offer a boutique photography experience. Personal attention is our specialty, so we take time to get to know each client in order to create unique art for her home.

What would you like customers to know about your business?
We solve the puzzle of how is this baby, child, family, dog or horse unique and how can we create beautiful portraits for their home.

What is your personal motto?
Wisdom wells within (found on a bracelet from my mom). I often wear it when I am a bundle of nerves and need a little extra encouragement.

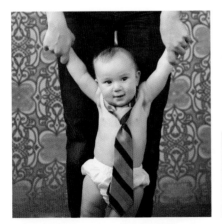

Miroslavich Photography

413 Wacouta St, Ste 320, St Paul, 651.343.4823
miroslavichphotography.com

Playful. Creative. Fun-loving.
Miroslavich Photography is a full-service boutique photography studio specializing in compelling relationship portraiture. Melissa, an award-winning photographer, captures your family, children, and pets as they really are; whether that's silly, quiet, sassy or playful. She brings relationships to life in front of the camera, creating unique art for your home. Miroslavich Photography is "where eyes dance, dimples dip, hearts skip."

Brooke Freiborg and Deb Amorde

Q&A

What makes your business unique?
High performance meets high
style at Moxie Cycling Co.

What is your favorite part of
being an entrepreneur?
We love being able to channel our
passion into a meaningful venture for
not only ourselves, but all the women
who share our love of cycling.

What is the best advice you've been given?
DA: Think big, start small and work fast.
BF: There is no time like the present.

What do you CRAVE?
Life-work balance and an abundance
of great relationships.

Moxie Cycling Co.

612.803.0464
moxiecycling.com

Stylish. Performance. Quality.
Moxie Cycling Co. is a cycling apparel company made by and for women with moxie. In a male-dominated sport where traditional men's jerseys are often simply modified for women, Moxie Cycling is evolving the world of women's cycling apparel by placing a woman's unique needs at the forefront of their design. Moxie Cycling believes women should never have to sacrifice performance, comfort or style.

My Sister & I, Inc.

952.461.1918
mysisterandiinc.com

Highly regarded. Innovative. Artistic
Sisters Jennifer and Julie of My Sister & I, Inc. have spent the last 12 years transforming
plain walls into exceptional works of art. They have earned a reputation for creating
spectacular custom European and decorative wall finishes. Using the finest materials,
My Sister and I has curated an extensive portfolio of finishes, including classic old
world European plasters as well as contemporary and modern wall designs.

Q&A

What makes your business unique?
All of our projects are one of a kind. It
is like starting a new job every time.

What would you like customers to
know about your business?
We ensure the finish chosen is an
appropriate choice for our customer's
home or business. We help them
avoid getting caught up in the latest
trend that they may regret later.

What can't you simply live
without in your business?
My sister, coffee and a trowel.

What is your biggest motivator?
Seeing our wall finishes on TV and
in local and national publications. We
must be doing something right!

Jennifer Wight and Julie Driscoll

Q&A

What would you like customers to know about your business?
We don't just sell skimpy bikinis! We are a store for real women with real bodies. Take a leap of faith and trust us. You will love the results.

What advice would you give women who are starting a business?
Humble thyself, you will make many mistakes and you are not the smartest woman ever. Start small and keep expenses to a minimum. Avoid expensive build-outs that do not directly increase revenue.

What is your personal motto?
"Fearless and Fabulous!" I am not afraid to take risks and I strive to ensure everything I do is classy and fabulous.

Jennifer Cermak

Nani Nalu Beachwear Boutique

50th & France, Edina, 952.546.5598
naninaluswim.com, Twitter: @NaniNalu

A-go-go. Astute. Alluring.
Nani Nalu provides a one-on-one shopping experience to help customers find the perfect fitting swimsuit. Why the personal shopper? The fit experts' knowledge of store products enables them to pull recommendations based on bust, pant, torso height, body shape, age of/any kids and activity level. This ensures that you try on the right sizes in the fitting room and helps select flattering styles for your body shape.

Debbie Bradley

Q&A

What makes your business unique?
We love creating the next "must have" for your home. Each treasure from us is a one-of-a-kind item for you.

What would you like customers to know about your business?
Our design team is ready for anything. You dream it, we create it. With our experienced and talented design team, we can make it happen for you.

What can't you simply live without in your business?
Being surrounded by such amazing people. The energy level is always so high around the store. I truly enjoy working with my boys and loyal staff; they are my family.

Natures Harvest

320 E Wayzata Blvd, Wayzata, 952.473.4687
naturesharvesthome.com, Twitter: @naturesharvest1

Nostalgic. Ever-changing. Thriving.
Natures Harvest opened on historic Lake Street in Wayzata, Minn. in 1992. Within
a few years, Natures Harvest moved to a more spacious location on Wayzata
Boulevard. Natures Harvest has been a thriving European-inspired boutique for
almost two decades. The design team at Natures Harvest travels the world to find
vintage gifts, distinctive accessories and furnishings for your home. Designers
are also available for fresh flowers, silk arrangements and potting services.

Photos by Giliane E. Mansfeldt Photography

Nelli Designs

612.669.8769
nellidesigns.com, Twitter: @nellidesigns

Heartfelt. Unique. Passionate.
Nelli Designs was born out of Kathy Kuhl's need for a memorial when she lost
her first dog Maggie in 2008. Kathy poured herself a candle to create a place to
hang Maggie's old collar and tags. Since then, Kathy has hand poured thousands
of grass-scented eco-soya candles, personalizing each order with collars and
custom tags. They're now a popular gift for any pet lover on any occasion.

Kathy Kuhl

Q&A

What would you like customers to know about your business?
While the business was inspired by my first dog Maggie, I offer gift and memorial candles for cat and horse lovers as well. Proceeds from sales support local and national rescue groups.

What is your favorite part of being an entrepreneur?
For years, I worked in advertising for brands that I didn't connect with personally. But now I own a brand that's making a difference in areas I'm passionate about.

What advice would you give women who are starting a business?
Do something that matters to you and to others. When I realized others also shared the need to honor their pets, I knew I had a solid business idea and the opportunity to fill a niche in the marketplace.

Nicole Fae

Q&A

What makes your business unique?
I use each client's individual look as my inspiration for beauty. Every client walks away feeling confident and beautiful, but most importantly, they feel like themselves.

What is your favorite part of being an entrepreneur?
There's no better feeling than knowing that I made a difference in someone's day. The confidence I see in a woman's eyes is better than any paycheck!

What is the best advice you've been given?
To just be me.

What or who inspires you?
My clients, many of whom are also female entrepreneurs, inspire me with their ambition, their determination and their strength. They motivate me to go after my dreams.

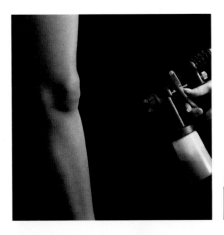

Photos by Chris McDuffie Photography except middle detail by Taylor Tupy Photography

Nicole Fae

275 E Fourth St, Studio 510, St Paul, 952.292.4775
nicolefae.com, Twitter: @MUANicoleFae

Artistic. Stylish. Honest.
Nicole Fae is the Twin Cities' one-stop beauty expert. Specializing in makeup, hairstyling, wardrobe, brow-shaping and custom airbrush tanning, since 2005 she has helped women look and feel their best. In 2010, Nicole Fae launched her own cosmetics line, featuring products custom-designed to highlight women's natural beauty. Her mission: to empower women to embrace whatever makes them beautiful. No matter what service they choose, they all leave with confidence.

NONTOXIQUE BEAUTY

888.869.4783
nontoxique.com, Twitter: @nontoxique

Holistic. Performance. Luxury.
NONTOXIQUE is a unique lifestyle brand created exclusively for the spa industry, with a niche focus on preserving the health and beauty of the hands, feet and nails, holistically. NONTOXIQUE captures the essence of today's active, savvy women and their aspired way of life in a way that is authentic and fun, natural and luxurious. NONTOXIQUE can be found in luxury spas around the country.

Photos by B Johnson Photos

Sheila Fredriksen

Q&A

What makes your business unique?
We're the first authentically natural, holistically formulated skin care line for the hands, feet and nails. The line is created by an industry manicurist, with a fresh and purposeful perspective.

What is your favorite part of being an entrepreneur?
I set the rules. In the world of NONTOXIQUE our No. 1 rule is that every day must be a fun adventure. If the day feels off, take the day off!

What is the best advice you've been given?
Go with your gut and always be authentic. Even if it takes longer to get where you want to be, people will respect you in the long run.

What is your personal motto?
Why follow when you can take the lead?

Susan Sun

Q&A

What would you like customers to know about your business?
Our brand mix includes both local talent and luxury designers that hail from the fashion capitals of the world.

What advice would you give women who are starting a business?
Before you sign on the line, ask yourself if you are ready to eat, breath, sleep, sweat and cry your business, because that is what it takes to be successful.

What is your biggest motivator?
Owning a business has always been my dream ever since I was little; owning a women's boutique is like icing on the cake.

What is your personal motto?
Be a leader, not a follower.

OPM Boutique

3700 Grand Way, St Louis Park, 952.567.7399
opmboutique.com, Twitter: @opmboutique

Upscale. Up-and-coming. Friendly.
OPM boutique follows a vision to always advocate the best in style, fashion and design to create an exciting customer experience. This hybrid boutique brings an atmosphere of big city style to the Twin Cities. OPM Boutique presents a place for emerging designers to showcase their collections alongside established industry leaders. You'll find fresh, versatile styles that span the spectrum of fashion.

Photos by Darin Back Photography

Kristi Pamperin

Q&A

What makes your business unique?
"Paper Miniskirt" is an anagram of my name. I love that it is quirky and makes readers stop and think. I didn't want a plain company name. It's definitely unique!

What would you like customers to know about your business?
I am insanely passionate about retrospection. I believe it is important to keep photographs around from all stages of life so you can look back on yourself, your accomplishments and celebrate them every single day.

What can't you simply live without in your business?
Fun, trendy fabrics. I am addicted to fabric shopping online. I don't sew, so this is my way of getting to experience the luxury of color and fiber!

Paper Miniskirt

320.250.1848
paperminiskirt.com, Twitter: @Paperminiskirt

Simple. Chic. Funky.
Kristi Pamperin combined her passions for retrospection, scrapbooking, color and organization, and her addiction to unique home decor items to create super chic Paper Miniskirt magnetic memo boards. Hang them up to organize your photographs, notes, quotes or coupons as a chic alternative to a cork board. Originally offering the memo boards online, Kristi now also sells at major retail and wholesale shows around the Midwest.

Photos by Shannon Tacheny of Feather Blue Studios

styled OCCASIONS

Paperista

5023 France Ave, Minneapolis, 612.886.3470
paperista.com, Twitter: @paperista

Stylish. Lovely. Distinctive.
Paperista is a stylish stationery and design boutique located at 50th & France
with awe-inspiring invitations and luxe paper goods for wedding, baby, social and
business clients. The fresh and modern store offers a carefully curated selection
of über stylish greeting cards, invitations, stationery, customized specialty gifts,
and entertaining accessories from their favorite vendors around the globe.

Q&A

What would you like customers to know about your business?
Paperista is the destination for anyone hosting an event. Our team is comprised of graphic designers and stylists who freely lend their design expertise to every client who walks in our doors.

What can't you simply live without in your business?
Customers exclaim everyday that they can't get enough of letterpress printed paper. Paperista thrives on the unanimous love of artisan printed paper!

What is your personal motto?
"It's the little things that make the big picture." I've lived by that statement for years! It's the reason I started Paperista.

Antoinette Ramos

Pam Mondale

Q&A

What makes your business unique?
It's all about peace and love.

What is your favorite part of being an entrepreneur?
The opportunity to collaborate with other creative people is always inspiring for me; I love that.

What advice would you give women who are starting a business?
Have integrity, follow through, stay focused, pay your bills on time, and make sure you are passionate about what you're doing.

What or who inspires you?
I'm inspired by the possibility of spreading peace—one t-shirt at a time.

What do you CRAVE?
Knowledge.

peace
pavilion

Peace Pavilion

Inside Guild Collective: 4414 Excelsior Blvd, St Louis Park, 952.378.1815
Underwood Street at the Minnesota State Fair
peace-pavilion.com, Twitter: @PeacePavilionMN

Groovy. Soulful. Funky.
Looking for a way to embrace your inner flower child? Peace Pavilion is
it! If you missed their psychedelic tent at the State Fair, fear not... you can
also find them at Guild Collective. More than a t-shirt shop, Peace Pavilion
carries jewelry, home decor, original art, vintage, and groovy novelties.
You'll love the shopping and may experience a flashback or two.

Lynn Gordon

Q&A

What makes your business unique?
Customers tell us they just love being in
our space. We created a haven to just sit
and "be." We provide free Wi-Fi all day,
comforting spaces and a welcoming bar.
Our customers love the taste of our water!
We went to great expense to install a special
water purification system offering pure
ambient, pure chilled and pure sparkling
water. Guests can help themselves
and fill up their own water bottles.

What would you like customers to
know about your business?
We were voted Best Vegetarian Cafe by
Minneapolis.St.Paul magazine our first
year. We enable customers to customize
their coffee drinks by offering almond milk,
hemp milk, rice milk, soy milk and coconut
milk. We only sweeten with organic agave.

Peoples Organic Coffee & Wine Cafe

3545 Galleria, Edina, 952.426.1856
peoplesorganic.com

Hip. Innovative. Inviting.
Peoples Organic is all about fresh, local, organic and sustainable, casual food served in a setting that is very Parisian. They began as an organic coffee concept cafe serving baked goods made fresh on site. Their wine bar and local artisan draft beers are essential complements to their small-batch roasted, fair-trade, organic espresso drinks. Blue cheese stratas and goat cheese omelets are served all day, along with nurturing soups, organic salads and artisan grilled sandwiches.

Photos by B Johnson Photos

Petalum

612.385.1399
petalum.com, Twitter: @petalumfloral

Meaningful. Enjoyable. Detailed.
Petalum was created by two seemingly opposite girls with one perfect thing in common:
a love for flowers. Sarah and Rebecca are inspired by the beauty of flowers and
encouraged by the endless possibilities. They design and create floral arrangements for
private parties, corporate events and weddings. From the initial consult to the big event,
Petalum is completely dedicated to their customers. They wouldn't have it any other way.

Main photo and middle detail by Ellierose Photography, portrait and left detail by Jacki V. Photography, right detail by Andrew Vick Photography

Rebecca Ross and Sarah Bauer

Q&A

What makes your business unique?
We recently launched a donation program
called Petalum Gives Back. We donate
a portion of our profits to the charity
of the bride and groom's choice.

**What can't you simply live
without in your business?**
A knife, tape, music and a little sugar.

**What advice would you give women
who are starting a business?**
Set goals and constantly revisit them to
ensure you are heading in the right direction.

What do you CRAVE?
Kisses from our kids, a warm summer
day, a night out with our husbands and
that extra detail that makes it just right.

Cassidy Lexcen

Q&A

What is your favorite part of being an entrepreneur?
Taking pride in what I have created and offer to clients. When clients comment on how much they enjoy our cozy, stylish space, it makes me so happy to know that they are having a wonderful experience.

What advice would you give women who are starting a business?
It takes a lot of time and devotion! It's not something you can walk away from when you want to—and there will be late nights. Perseverance and time are key.

What is your biggest motivator?
Bills are usually a great motivator! I always ask myself, "how far can I go? What more can I do? Can I make my big dreams a reality?"

Phatchellies

11 10th Ave S, Hopkins, 952.938.5402
phatchellies.com

Chic. Vivacious. Indulgent.
Phatchellies is one of the best-kept secrets in the Twin Cities area. A little
hidden gem in downtown Hopkins, it is one of the most up-and-coming
salons in the metro. Phatchellies features some of most talented, highly
trained technicians who offer the best of hair, skin and nail services.
Featured lines are Kerastse, Bumble and bumble and Epicuren.

Planet Spirit, Inc.

840 Decatur Ave N, Golden Valley, 763.512.1638
planetspirit.com

Friendly. Active. Competitive.
Planet Spirit, located in Golden Valley, Minn. is a cheerleading, dance, tumbling and stunting training facility. Planet Spirit offers classes, camps and team programs for males and females of all ability levels, ages 4 to adult. Planet Spirit "All Star" team members have been featured on Kare 11, "Good Morning America" and ESPN.

Sue Godes

Q&A

What makes your business unique?
Competitive cheerleading has grown
in popularity over the years. With
12 competitive "All Star" teams and
many classes, Planet Spirit offers a
unique, athletic way to get involved.

What would you like customers to
know about your business?
The staff at Planet Spirit strive to not only
teach competitive cheerleading, but also
many other valuable life lessons. They enjoy
offering a "family environment" for all.

What is your favorite part of
being an entrepreneur?
My favorite aspect of this business over
the years is having the ability to work
closely with such wonderful people
and establishing relationships with
the amazing athletes and parents!

Katie McShane and Lois Eliason

Q&A

What would you like customers to
know about your business?
Each Post- handbag and accessory
is part of a limited edition
handcrafted by master artisans.

What is your favorite part of
being an entrepreneur?
Bringing an outrageous idea to the table
without fear that it might be shut down.

What is the best advice you've been given?
Stop beating your heads against the
wall by trying to do everything. Focus on
your strengths and you'll find that things
will start falling into place for you.

What or who inspires you?
We're always inspired by renegade artists
and art movements. Anything that is edgy
and outsider gets a double take from us.

Post-

postdash.com, Twitter: @Post_Style

Art-inspired. Luxe. Smart.
Post- handbags and accessories are unique, fashionable and accessible.
Co-founders Lois Eliason and Katie McShane use their training as art
historians to guide them in their creative process. Each collection by
Post- pays tribute to key artists, works and trends from diverse periods
in history. Hugely popular, the first three collections are inspired by the
Italian Renaissance, 1960s Pop art and the Industrial Revolution.

Main photo by Stephanie Hynes Photography. Portrait by Mandy Birdwell,
middle detail by Joan Buccina, left and right detail by Lois Eliason

Pumpz & Company

3335 Galleria, Edina, 952.926.2252
pumpzco.com, Twitter: @pumpzco

Fashionable. Unique. Inviting.
Pumpz & Company is the place to find your future favorites—shoes, handbags,
jewelry, accessories—with a helpful and experienced staff. Pumpz & Company
buyers travel the world to discover classic and trend-right styles to fit your
lifestyle. Located in Edina Galleria, Pumpz & Company is a convenient, fun
shopping experience that will change the way you accessorize!

Photos by B Johnson Photos

#

Marlys Badzin (standing
middle) with her staff

Q&A

What makes your business unique?
We travel to Milan, Paris, and Tel Aviv to find
products that aren't represented locally.

What is your favorite part of
being an entrepreneur?
After 13 years in this business, the best
part has to be the relationships that I've
built with vendors, customers and staff.

What is the best advice you've been given?
You don't have to do it all yourself.
Surround yourself with talented
people who complement each other
and the needs of the business.

What is the biggest perk about
owning a small business?
Staying up on fashion and trends keeps me
young—and I love having an inside view of
what people will be wearing next season!

Q&A

What would you like customers to
know about your business?
Friends and family make the world go
round. So tell them! Often! Our app
helps make relationships stronger
with the ease of technology and the
grace of stylish correspondence.

What can't you simply live
without in your business?
Our team. I am constantly awed and
humbled by the talent that is our company.
Creative, lovely people who love what
we do and love who we do it with.

What is the best advice you've been given?
To succeed, you don't have to be right
every time, you just have to be right more
often than you are wrong. Don't be afraid
to leap. Be afraid of standing still.

Erin Newkirk

Photos by Kara Kurth

Red Stamp

redstamp.com, Twitter: @redstamp

Modern. Personal. Mobile.
Red Stamp believes sending correspondence is not only good form, it's also just plain nice. With the rise of e-everything, there are so many more ways to communicate than ever before—which is why Red Stamp developed an amazing app. Now you can text, email, post on Facebook, tweet and/or mail gorgeous paper postcards right from your mobile device. The Red Stamp app has been featured in *Real Simple*, *InStyle*, *Matchbook* magazine and more.

Christy Johnson

What would you like customers to know about your business?
I'm a one-stop shop. I do the concept and design work, as well as coordinate printing and pick up and delivery of the final product. I make the process easy.

What can't you simply live without in your business?
My open-minded clients! They tell me their stories and let me run wild with my imagination. It's so fun to transform their details and personalities into a stylish, customized design.

What is your personal motto?
Keep print alive! There is nothing like the tactile nature of a paper invitation to communicate that the event will be special. Plus, who doesn't like getting something cool—and not junk mail—in their mailbox?

redshoes26 design

612.695.4366
redshoes26design.com, Twitter: @redshoes26

Clean. Stylish. Imaginative.
redshoes26 design is a full-service creative resource that specializes in custom wedding and event invitation suites, branding and greeting cards. Owner Christy Johnson uses her skills as a graphic designer, illustrator and typography nerd to create one-of-a-kind designs for clients who are looking for something that expresses exactly who they are. She is often told that her wedding suite designs are "unlike anything else out there."

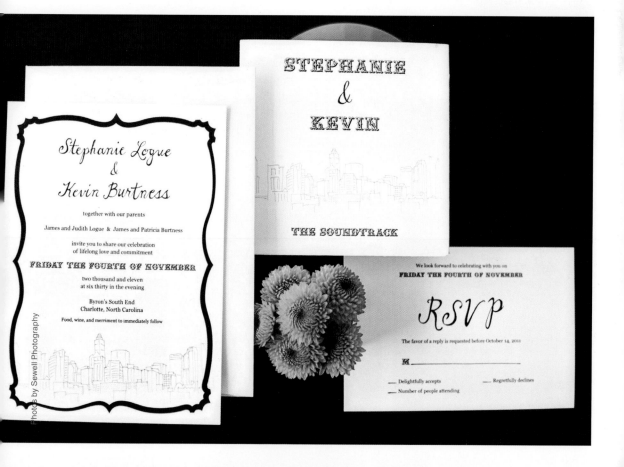

Jennifer Kroeger

Q&A

What makes your business unique?
Traveling with my father to antique shows across the country allows me to collect one-of-a-kind items for my designs from diverse places.

What is the best advice you've been given?
Get to know others in your field. Having great connections will be an asset throughout your business.

What or who inspires you?
Sitting in my studio with parts and pieces from across the country and creating unique, new designs with items that would have otherwise been forgotten.

What do you CRAVE?
Digging through piles of vintage pieces, never knowing what kind of inspiration I will get from the items I pick out.

Relic Charm

651.235.6567
reliccharm.com, Twitter: @reliccharm

Feminine. Unique. Vintage.
Relic Charm uses vintage pieces to create jewelry with a fresh, new look
that pairs beautifully with today's fashions. From statement pieces to your
everyday signature necklace, Relic Charm can satisfy your craving. Selling at
local events and shops around town, Relic Charm also holds an occasional
sale as J & E Antiques in Saint Paul where they offer vintage home decor.

Robin Fisher

Q&A

What makes your business unique?
I acquire the stones and agates from
India and Brazil, then string the perfect
combination of beads all on a leather cord.

What would you like customers to
know about your business?
I have experience. For more than a decade
I lent my style expertise to retail giants. I
traveled to fashion capitals of the world,
all the while cultivating my eye for design
that I now use for my own jewelry line.

What is your favorite part of
being an entrepreneur?
The ability to make my own decisions;
to make my own mistakes; to learn
something new every day; and to
meet and work with incredibly talented
people who support my vision.

Robin Fisher Jewelry

612.850.3851
robinfisherjewelry.com

Original. Stunning. Distinctive.
From the beginning, Robin's love for accessories, specifically jewelry, fueled an entrepreneurial spirit that she tapped into after leaving Target Corporation to raise her three children. Robin recalls taking apart some of her own necklaces and playing around with the pieces. The result was a sliced agate necklace strung on a leather cord—and the inspiration for the Robin Fisher Jewelry line.

What do you CRAVE?

" *To always be challenged —
it's what keeps me
learning and growing.* "

Laurie Pyle of Cocoa & Fig

St. Paul Farmers' Market by Elijah Parker

Owners Beth Griesgraber and Jessica
Strong with Judy McCoy (middle)

Q&A

What makes your business unique?
Everything in the store is a sensory delight...
the scent of a burning candle, the touch of
a spa robe, lace of the lingerie, all of it.

What is your favorite part of
being an entrepreneur?
We are living our dream. We are proud
our children will grow up learning by our
example that dreams can come true!

What advice would you give women
who are starting a business?
Own your business before you actually
open your door: live, breathe, talk, believe,
love your creation. By living it, you will be
trustworthy to your customer. We live to love.

What is your personal motto?
Love is contagious.

Room No. 3

4948 France Ave S, Edina, 952.746.3003
roomno3.com

Sophisticated. Subtle. Luxe.
Step into Room No. 3 and be transported to a relaxing retreat... a place where
you can lounge and love in simple luxury. Room No. 3 masters the idea of subtle
sexiness with their collections of lingerie and loungewear. Room No. 3 offers
all displayed decor and accessories for sale, so, whether your heart craves a
new treat for yourself, your love, or your home, you'll find it at Room No. 3.

Photos by Cadence Cornelius

Main photo and right detail by Callahan & Company
Photography additional photos by Matt Blum

Rox Minneapolis Jewelry

2205 California St NE, Studio 403, Minneapolis, 612.834.5027
roxmpls.com, Twitter: @roxmplsjewelry

Exotic. Sensuous. Sophisticated.
There's no other jewelry quite like Rox— each piece is handcrafted with gemstones
sourced from exotic locations. Our philosophy is to heighten your natural bond
with the earth. Rox uses the finest artisan metals to create a luxurious look.
Featured in *Redbook* magazine and on "The Tyra Banks Show," Rox is found
in boutiques and fine jewelers throughout the Twin Cities metro area.

Q&A

What makes your business unique?
Rox designs are exclusive,
one-of-a-kind treasures.

What would you like customers to
know about your business?
Rox Jewelry is sold in 22 boutiques
and jewelers worldwide.

What can't you simply live
without in your business?
Travel. It's what makes Rox unique.
Our stones are sourced from
wonderful bazaars, shopping districts
and peddlers around the globe.

What is the best advice you've been given?
Never give up.

What is your biggest motivator?
Not accepting failure.

Robyne Robinson

Gilah Mashaal

Q&A

What makes your business unique?
Each invitation is custom created for
the individual event and client. No
cookie-cutter invites here! Set the first
impression of your life's special moments
with an invitation from Save the Date.

What would you like customers to
know about your business?
I provide a personalized service with every
event I handle. I craft every piece with only
the most beautiful high-quality papers and
printing processes. It's all eye candy!

What is your personal motto?
James Michener once said, "I love
the swirl and swing of words as they
tangle with human emotions."

What or who inspires you?
Color, swirly fonts and the
clients I am creating for.

MR. AND MRS. MICHAEL RODICH
REQUEST THE HONOR OF YOUR PRESENCE
AT THE MARRIAGE OF THEIR DAUGHTER

Jessica Elizabeth

Zachary Ben

SON OF MR. AND MRS. TODD FREEMAN

SUNDAY, THE THIRD OF JULY
TWO THOUSAND AND ELEVEN
AT FIVE THIRTY IN THE AFTERNOON

ADATH JESHURUN CONGREGATI[...]
10500 HILLSIDE LANE
MINNETONK[...]

Jessica Elizabeth Rodich
and
Zachary Ben Freeman

ADATH JESHURUN CONGREGATIO[...]
MINNETONKA, MINN[...]

Save the Date

612.269.0763
savethedateinvites.com, Twitter: @savedateinvites

Gorgeous. Unique. Personal.
Save the Date creates impeccable custom invitations with concierge-
quality service. Distinctive, beautifully crafted invitations from Save the
Date are the perfect opening act to your special moment, adding flair and
panache or understated elegance to weddings, bar mitzvahs, birthday
celebrations, baby announcements or graduation parties. Save the Date
tailors every invitation to match your personal style and budget.

199

Sewell Photography

612.799.1245
sewellphotography.com, Twitter: @sewellphoto

Captivating. Authentic. Timeless.
Sewell Photography is an award-winning boutique photography studio
specializing in on-site documentary and lifestyle photography, including
weddings, engagement, post-wedding, expectant mother, child and family
photo sessions. Jennie's photographs are often seen in local and national
magazines and blogs. Sewell Photography is based in Minneapolis and is
available for travel worldwide.

Q&A

What makes your business unique?
You will be getting my personal attention to detail at every stage of the process, from the first phone call or email to the final editing of your photographs.

What would you like customers to know about your business?
Years of experience have taught me how to deal with the most challenging photography situations. My clients trust that I can capture the unique beauty in every subject and setting.

What is your biggest motivator?
I want to tell my subject's story in an honest and beautiful way.

What do you CRAVE?
Color and light!

Jennie Sewell

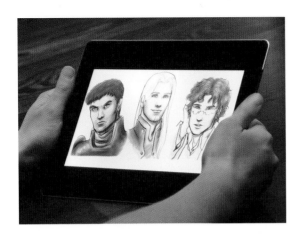

Q&A

What makes your business unique?
We create games for women who
want to change the world.

What would you like customers to
know about your business?
The majority of our team is
female. We're women creating
entertainment for our sisters, mothers,
daughters, nieces and friends.

What can't you simply live
without in your business?
Social media. The support we get
from our Twitter and Facebook
fans means the world to us.

What is your favorite part of
being an entrepreneur?
Watching a project come to life right
before our eyes and then watching it
grow into something more beautiful
than we could have ever imagined.

What advice would you give women
who are starting a business?
Don't be afraid to ask for help! You'll be
surprised by how many people truly want
to help you and see you succeed.

Jacqueline Urick and Elizabeth Tupper

SieEnt

612.810.5888
sieent.com, Twitter: @SieEnt

Inspiring. Delightful. Fun.
SieEnt (pronounced SEE-ent) develops and designs engaging video games with women in mind for your personal computer, mobile phone and game consoles. They release games in an episodic format. Like your favorite TV show, each episode provides 60 to 90 minutes of play time. Their first title, a five episode 2D science fiction murder mystery, is set to release in early 2012.

Skin Therapease

1907 E Wayzata Blvd, #120, Wayzata, 952.404.0000
skintherapease.com

Healthy. Sincere. Energized.
Skin Therapease's philosophy is preventive and proactive skin care with emphasis on age management. They offer a full-service skin health and skin care clinic. Skin Therapease takes great pride to encourage a holistic approach, which includes consideration to products, ingredients, customized services, diet, enviromental issues and lifestyles. Other services include: photo-rejuvenation, laser resurfacing, profractional, skin tightening, laser hair reduction, vascular, Botox and injections.

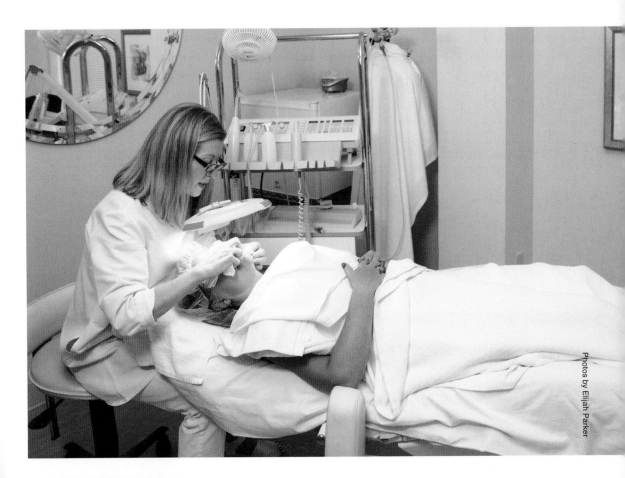

Pat Scherven

Q&A

What would you like customers to know about your business?
We are here for our clients' and customers' skin care needs, considering all skin care options.

What can't you simply live without in your business?
The opportunity to grow.

What is the best advice you've been given?
Follow your passion, and focus.

What is your biggest motivator?
Happy clients!

What do you CRAVE?
I would like to set the highest of standards in the skin health/care arena, letting clients know that we are focused on their best skin care interests.

Martha McCarthy & Emily Pritchard

Q&A

What makes your business unique?
Our flexibility in service offerings, attention to the unique needs of each client, and out-of-the box creativity that cuts through the clutter and makes a splash!

What would you like customers to know about your business?
We're addicted. As social media addicts, we can't help but stay on top of the ever-changing world of social media. Our knowledge in this space has been very valuable to clients.

What advice would you give women who are starting a business?
Be a fearless female. Refuse to sit back and simply watch the world turn. Do what you love. Make a difference.

Who is your role model or mentor?
Ann Winblad: UST alumna, experienced entrepreneur and fearless female. She's one brilliant badass.

What is your personal motto?
"Find something you love to do and you'll never have to work a day in your life."
—Harvey MacKay

The Social Lights

651.962.4551
thesocial-lights.com, Twitter: @SocialLightUp

Fresh. Fun. Strategic.
The Social Lights take a creative approach to social media, business communications and event marketing. This innovative marketing agency assists companies as they dive into digital by infusing creativity into custom campaigns made exclusively for the Web. They are experts at integrating the physical (location and live events) with the digital (online presence) to create highly dynamic marketing campaigns.

Stacia Wilson and Sarah Kurn Skincare

86 Mahtomedi Ave, Mahtomedi, 651.426.6040
staciawilsonskincare.net, sarahkurnskincare.com, Twitter: @stacia_skincare

Specialized. Expert. Passionate.
Stacia Wilson and Sarah Kurn Skincare is a unique skin boutique. When you walk in, you enter a girly shop with all the must-have skincare and makeup products. They recommend getting one of their amazing, results-driven skin care treatments before starting a skin care regime. They then customize a facial that is right for you with peels, microdermabrasion or oxygen therapy.

Stacia Wilson and Sarah Kurn

Q&A

What makes your business unique?
We are the in-between place for those people who want more than a spa facial, but don't want the clinical walls of a dermatology office.

What would you like customers to know about your business?
It is not just a day at the "spa." The treatments are indulgent, but most importantly, you see results. The knowledge and tools are given to make that happen.

What advice would you give women who are starting a business?
Follow your instincts and stay true to your beliefs.

What is your biggest motivator?
When someone comes in and says that a complete stranger told them that their skin looks great.

Becky Sturm

Q&A

What makes your business unique?
All beauty and grooming products
have my personal stamp of approval.
3waybeauty products were blind-
tested by a salon and my friends and
family for complete effectiveness.

What would you like customers to
know about your business?
The design, manufacturing and printing
for 3waybeauty is all done locally. Our
packaging is 100 percent compostable,
recyclable and is manufactured at a
family-owned mill that runs on 100
percent hydro-electric power.

Who is your role model or mentor?
The female small business community
here in the Twin Cities. These women have
given me so much love and support during
these recession years. It is immeasurable!

StormSister Spatique

612.716.5480
stormsister.biz, Twitter: @StormSister

3waybeauty

612.716.5480
3waybeauty.com, Twitter: @3waybeauty

Expert. Sassy. Distinctive.
StormSister Spatique is an online beauty shopping experience that carries lotions, potions and serums for hair, skin, nails and body. Owner and founder Becky Sturm, a beauty industry maven who grew up in the salon and spa industry, is also the inventor of the three-way shampoo, shower and shave grooming bar shhh. Wanna try a three-way?

Photos courtesy of StormSister Spatique

Studio C Designs

6005 Wayzata Blvd, Ste 100, St Louis Park, 952.797.7777
studiocjewelry.com, Twitter: @sarad123

Custom. Exquisite. Luxury.
Studio C Designs is a boutique custom jeweler featuring one-of-a-kind collections
of colorful gem and pearl jewelry in precious metals. At Studio C Designs, each
piece is handcrafted on the premises to customer specification and all fine goods
and products are sourced ethically. Studio C Designs offers personal services
for engraving, repairs, antique restoration of jewelry and appraisal services.

Sara D. Commers

◗ Q&A

What makes your business unique?
Studio C Designs uniquely creates
and builds all jewelry designs in-house
using modern technology and ethically
sourced gems, metals and pearls,
by JA Certified Bench Jewelers.

What can't you simply live
without in your business?
In my business, I cannot live without
my laser welder; as a business
philosophy, I couldn't live without fun
and laughter in the workplace.

What or who inspires you?
I am inspired by the dynamic women leaders
I know in business and in the jewelry
industry who juggle business, social and
family while living their lives to the fullest!

Christina Holm-Sandok

Q&A

What makes your business unique?
We work both with businesses and individuals. People have brand images just like companies—we are here to help define it.

What would you like customers to know about your business?
Our team is built of discerning women with media relations, marketing, lifestyle editorial, merchandising and event planning experience. Our diverse backgrounds allow us to give our clients well-rounded service.

Who is your role model or mentor?
My grandmother. She was a hardworking entrepreneur with a great reputation and an amazing wardrobe!

What is your personal motto?
Like a swan, we're graceful on top and paddling like crazy underneath.

Style-Architects

612.326.9020
style-architects.com, Twitter: @StyleArchitects

Chic. Sophisticated. Modern.
Style-Architects offers stylish services for the modern business and sophisticate. With a wealth of experience, they are a local "dream team" that offers public relations, marketing, event planning, concierge and wardrobe styling services. The creative team consists of Christina Holm-Sandok, Elizabeth Plaetz Lori, Ranosha Coffelt and Kelly Showalter.

Photos by Canary Grey Photography

Q&A

What makes your business unique?
I'm known as the jack-of-all-trades, as Style-Infused Living is not just an interior design house. You can also hire Style-Infused Living for home and office organization, event planning, styling, landscaping design... you name it.

What is your favorite part of being an entrepreneur?
Watching my business evolve and take shape in new ways every day. Following my passion for all things design. It's exciting to create something from scratch and watch it grow.

What is the best advice you've been given?
Be bold and confident!

Cinda Pfeil

Style-Infused Living

952.484.2204
styleinfusedliving.com, Twitter: @styleinfusedliv

Genuine. Inspired. Tailored.
Style-Infused Living is a boutique interior design house providing custom design and
decorating, space planning and organization, and project management oversight.
Whether it's a personal touch to framed art, shaping a closet to show its beauty,
or coordinating wall colors to give life and flow to a home, Cinda Pfeil creates
and refines the essence of each unique project—infusing your life with style!

Q&A

What makes your business unique?
Every day is different. Every client and couple is unique. Every event is a once-in-a-lifetime occasion. There is no "typical day" at Table 6!

What would you like customers to know about your business?
It's all about them! My passion is turning their ideas, dreams and visions into incredible events that they are able to fully enjoy with their loved ones.

What is your favorite part of being an entrepreneur?
The thrill of every small success. You devote so much time, energy and passion into your business that every little victory is sweet.

Stephanie Johnson

Main photo by Happily Ever After Photography, portrait by Sewell Photography, left detail by Gina Lang Photography, middle detail by Emily Griffith Photography, right detail by Red Ribbon Studio

Table 6 Productions

651.785.6234
table6productions.com, Twitter: @Table6MN

Meticulous. Creative. Sophisticated.
Table 6 Productions is a boutique wedding and event planning company. Weddings are their specialty and their services extend to all personal events and special occasions. The planners at Table 6 act as confidantes, style connoisseurs, etiquette experts, financial advisors, personal assistants and detail divas—there to guide you through every step of planning the most memorable and unique event possible.

Tiger Athletics

612.695.8770
tigerathletics.com, Twitter: @TigerAthletics

Athletic. Authentic. Awe-Inspiring.
TIGER ATHLETICS is a high energy, mobile athletic company that provides unparalleled functional training programs for all ages. Co-founders Stacie and Chris Clark offer highly skilled, professional coaching within a dynamic, out-of-the-gym environment. TIGER ATHLETICS sets a completely new paradigm in athletic training. It is real. It is intense. It is training for life. TIGER ATHLETICS was awarded "Best Trainers in Twin Cities" by *Minnesota Monthly* magazine.

Q&A

What makes your business unique?
We are mobile and specialize in athletic development for youth and adults, from one-on-one to sports team training. Find us at various locations all over the Twin Cities through our many established partnerships.

What would you like customers to know about your business?
You get results. We understand training and we take you to the next level. Goals range from weight loss to improving pace, enhancing form/technique, or simply working to get quicker, faster, stronger, leaner and better.

What advice would you give women who are starting a business?
Be ready to be on call 24/7! It takes a lot longer than one thinks for an idea to come to fruition, but the journey is worth it.

Stacie Clark

Lisa Edevold

Q&A

What makes your business unique?
The whole restaurant is in a good mood. I truly love what I do, and this passion trickles into the staff, the food and the overall vibe of Tiger Sushi.

What would you like customers to know about your business?
Every sushi bar in the world gives you soy sauce. Yawn. At Tiger, your sushi comes with our signature homemade "Tosa" and lively "Tiger" sauces.

What is your biggest motivator?
Recognition. The words, "I love your restaurant," never get old. Having people enthusiastically respond to something that I created is what keeps me going.

What is your personal motto?
People matter. Not things.

Tiger Sushi

Mall of America, 952.876.9410
2841 Lyndale Ave S, Minneapolis, 612.874.1800
tigersushiusa.com

Bold. Fusion. Fresh.
Tiger Sushi opened at MOA in 2003, in the shadows of every major national chain store. And right away, this tiny, little indie sushi bar began shaking things up. Their playful, inventive approach to food combines flavors from all over the world, including Mediterranean, French, Thai and Indonesian. Tiger Sushi 2, the gorgeous full-service incarnation, opened in the edgy, ultra-hip Lyn-Lake neighborhood in 2007.

Unleash Your Inner Foodie

612.860.5961
unleashyourinnerfoodie.com, Twitter: @yourinnerfoodie

Creative. Fun. Memorable.
Unleash Your Inner Foodie is an online business that helps people create memorable experiences for their family and friends by combining great food with easy, fun entertaining. DeeAnn believes that food is the best setting for truly connecting with people. Their unique products and services help you achieve that simple, casual entertaining lifestyle we all want!

Q&A

What makes your business unique?
We make cooking and entertaining easy and fun like it's supposed to be! Our recipes, menus, entertaining tips and products get you out of the kitchen and into your party.

What is your favorite part of being an entrepreneur?
The ability to control my destiny. And traveling around the country to find great products and ideas to share with my customers to make their everyday entertaining easy and fun.

What advice would you give women who are starting a business?
Fasten your seatbelt, you're in for the ride of your life!

What is the best advice you've been given?
Never be afraid to ask for help.

DeeAnn McArdle

Kerry Ciardelli

Q&A

What makes your business unique?
Victory Home & Interiors is one of the only independent retail and design resources in the Twin Cities. I offer interior design services, furniture, lighting, rugs, antiques, accessories, books, jewelry, candles, bedding and gifts. Victory is the exclusive Twin Cities resource for Madeline Weinrib fabrics, Christopher Spitzmiller lamps and my own line of pillows and other home accessories.

What would you like customers to know about your business?
Victory Home & Interiors was inspired by my passion for travel and my love of beauty, style, entertaining, interior design, elegance, and all things vintage and modern.

VICTORY

3505 W 44th St, Minneapolis, 612.926.8200
shopvictory.com, Twitter: kerryciardelli

Elegant. Chic. On-trend
Established in 2003 by Kerry Ciardelli, interior designer and entrepreneur,
Victory Home & Interiors is a distinctive design studio and retail store
in Linden Hills, Minneapolis. Kerry's signature style combines antiques,
luxurious fabrics and modern pieces to create a look that's all her own.
Whether you're looking for a lovely hostess gift, a new piece of furniture
or an entirely new look for a beloved home, you'll find it at Victory.

Photos by Shannon Tacheny of Feather Blue Studios

Lorinda Judge Ims

Q&A

What makes your business unique?
The Vintage Jewelry Collection features unique, hard-to-find vintage jewelry. We provide an educational experience so our customers understand the historical importance of their pieces.

What would you like customers to know about your business?
We are a full-service jeweler with one of the largest selections of vintage costume and estate jewelry. We are focused on providing our customers with a fun and educational shopping experience.

Who is your role model or mentor?
My parents. My father worked three jobs to finish college when my sister, brothers and I were children. My mother showed me the beauty and history of vintage jewelry.

The Vintage Jewelry Collection

8 Third St NW, Osseo, 763.315.6577
thevintagejewelrycollection.com, Twitter: @VintageJewelCo

Edgy. Unique. Educated.
The Vintage Jewelry Collection showcases an array of pristine jewelry from the late 19th century to today. The collection is expertly curated from an expansive inventory that features designers whose contributions have shaped the jewelry industry. Vintage jewelry is a wearable work of art with history—it is a smart investment.

Volume Salon

4000 Annapolis Ln, Ste 104, Plymouth, 763.557.0896
volumesalon.com, Twitter: @Volume_Salon

Beautiful. Comfortable. Affordable.
Walking through the front door of Volume Salon will make you question if you are
really in west metro. The brand-new, cutting-edge decor and talented, friendly staff
will make you feel as if you just stepped into a NYC salon. Volume Salon offers high-
end hair services at affordable prices and top professional hair care products.

Jenny Leffring

Q&A

What advice would you give women who are starting a business?
Live, act and dress for the success you crave.

What is your biggest motivator?
Being a mother of four boys. I want them to see that their mother is a successful business woman and teach them a strong work ethic.

What is your personal motto?
"I say it, I be it!" My life will be what I make it and success is the only option.

What can't you simply live without in your business?
My husband! He is my rock. He keeps me focused and kicks my drive into high gear.

Write Away

612.822.0002
writeaway.com, Twitter: @WriteAwayPaper

Personalized. Special. Pretty.
For 15 years, Write Away has produced uniquely personalized stationery and
gifts with character and style. They are now delighted to offer customized
invitations and announcements for any occasion. Their holiday cards
are vibrant, creative and really make an exceptional statement.

Sarah Graff & Meredith Johnson

Q&A

What would you like customers to know about your business?
Our new line of custom invitations and announcements have expanded our capabilities. We accommodate your vision or help you create something special to set the tone for your event.

What is your favorite part of being an entrepreneur?
Working with a friend, providing meaningful opportunities for women to create balance in their lives and loving our products!

What or who inspires you?
People who take the time to write meaningful words on paper. We really treasure them as much or more than any other gift.

Yum! Kitchen and Bakery

4000 Minnetonka Blvd, St Louis Park, 952.922.4000
yumkitchen.com, Twitter: @YumKitchen

Yum. Homemade. Delicious.
Yum! Kitchen and Bakery is the ultimate neighborhood restaurant serving fresh and friendly food that makes you smile. The bakery offers award-winning cakes, cupcakes, oversized cookies, ever-changing morning pastries and fair-trade coffee. The kitchen prepares seasonal soups and salads, sandwiches and entrees. Favorites include chicken soup, gumbo, apple harvest salad, fancy-schmancy tuna melt, Hugo's Mahi tacos and Patticake, their signature chocolate cake with buttercream frosting.

Q&A

What makes your business unique?
Yum! is about happy people serving great homemade food. We love what we do and hope it shows.

What can't you simply live without in your business?
Passion, fresh food and hungry people.

What is the biggest perk about owning a small business?
Instant gratification... we think it, plan it and make it happen. If it goes well, it is a great feeling, if not, we learn, adapt and try again.

Who is your role model or mentor?
My parents are extraordinary. My mom is passionate and allowed me to make a mess in the kitchen. My dad is an entrepreneur and my instructor in business and life.

Patti Soskin

Pillsbury building by Elijah Parker

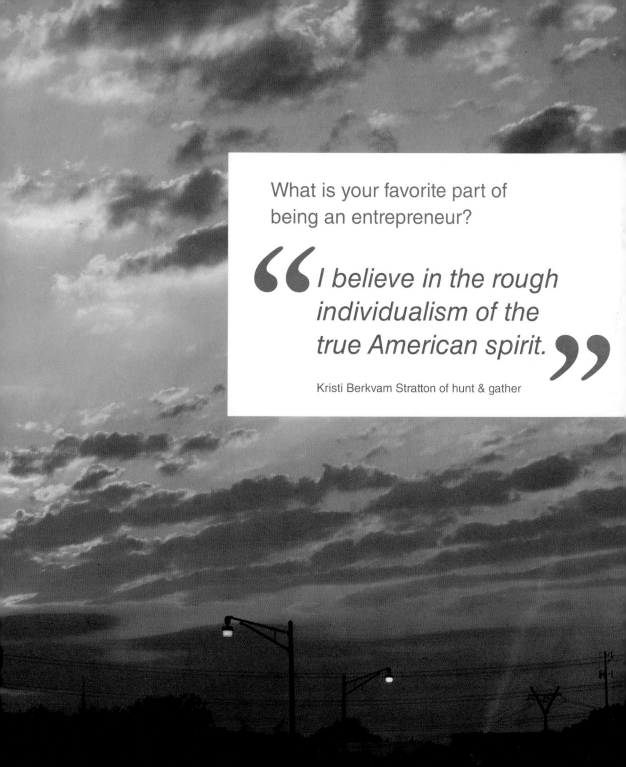

What is your favorite part of
being an entrepreneur?

" *I believe in the rough
individualism of the
true American spirit.* "

Kristi Berkvam Stratton of hunt & gather

Contributors

We believe in acknowledging, celebrating and passionately supporting locally owned businesses and entrepreneurs. We are extremely grateful to all contributors for this publication.

CRAVE Founder

Melody Biringer connects women in innovative ways so they can help each other pursue the lives they crave, in business and in pleasure.

thecravecompany.com
startupjunkie.com

MELODY BIRINGER

Innovative. Feminine. Connective.
Melody Biringer, self-avowed "start-up junkie," has built companies that range from Biringer Farm, a family-run specialty-food business, to home furnishings to a fitness studio.

Her current entrepreneurial love-child is The CRAVE Company, a network of businesses designed to creatively connect entrepreneurs who approach business in a fresh new way with the stylish consumers they desire. The CRAVE family includes CRAVEparty, CRAVEguides and CRAVEbusiness. What started out as girlfriends getting together for exclusive glam-gal gatherings, CRAVEparty has since expanded into CRAVEbusiness, a resource for entrepreneurs seeking a modern approach, and CRAVEguides, delivering style and substance. Since initially launching in Seattle, Melody has taken CRAVE to more than 30 cities worldwide, including New York City, Boston, Los Angeles, Chicago, Amsterdam and Toronto.

Melody is a loyal community supporter, versed traveler and strong advocate for women-owned businesses.

CRAVE Minneapolis Partner

kathy@backpocket.biz
backpocket.biz
Twitter: @backpocketbbf

KATHY HANSON

Discriminating. Energetic. Compassionate.
Kathy has been an entrepreneur for most of her professional life. With CRAVE, Kathy found the perfect opportunity to focus her passion for connecting women in the Twin Cities with local innovative and gutsy entrepreneurs to inspire, educate and empower one another.

With boundless enthusiasm for curating this book, Kathy's goal was to have Crave Minneapolis/St. Paul be a reflection of our city's passion for excellence, sustainability and distinction. Kathy's professional expertise came into play by helping each featured businesswoman strategically engage the reader with fabulous photos and enticing copy! Minneapolis/St. Paul has a wonderfully diverse community of innovative businesswomen supported by a community of discriminating shoppers, foodies, artists, athletes and philanthropists. It was Kathy's pleasure and honor to work with all the remarkable women in this book.

Contributors (continued)

Kenny Friedman
designer
smonkyou.com

By day, Kenny is a designer and creative director. By night, he writes the irreverant daddy blog smonkyou.com. He has been dubbed the one and only male mommy blogger—by himself—and the term has stuck. His blogging efforts led to Moosejaw naming a softshell jacket after him.

Staci Friedman
project manager

Staci is an organizational guru who enjoys her projects' finer details. She has planned more than 100 marketing events, social gatherings, weddings, and fundraisers around the world for high-profile clients. Her passions include being a Montessori teacher, shopping, eating out and making her son giggle.

Jennifer Sellers
editor
jennisellers@gmail.com

Jennifer is a freelance editor and writer with boundless enthusiasm for the written word, a passion for perfection and an eye for design. Jennifer can often be found dancing Argentine tango, playing croquet, dining out and shopping local.

Meredith Edstam
CRAVE Minneapolis intern

Meredith has always had a way with words, especially those written to express enthusiasm! She's excited to use her word weaving talents in the social media realm; to spread awareness for deserving people and businesses that may not be as eloquent and need a push to bring attention to their wares!

Rochagne Roux
CRAVE Minneapolis intern

South African girl Rochagne Roux is an aspiring fashion designer. She jumps to be a part of anything involved with style, fun and meeting new people. She is determined to follow her passion in the fashion world. She loves spending her time expressing her creativeness, staying active and searching for vintage keepsakes.

Darin Back
photographer
darinbackphoto.com

Born in Minnesota. Studied photography in college. Took lots of pictures. Made lots of contacts. Got a few breaks. Showed up. Didn't blow it. Got a job with Annie Leibovitz. Worked super hard. Shot snowboarding in Vail for five years. Headed back to Minneapolis to be around family. Can't imagine any other way of life.

Brenda Johnson
photographer
612.618.2022
bjohnsonphotos.com

Brenda has the ability to tell the visual story of a place, person or product. Her images display the victory of what's seen over what's not. Her photos have appeared in numerous publications and exhibitions, and are permanent installations around Minnesota and Wisconsin.

Giliane E. Mansfeldt
photographer
612.387.6181
giliane-e-mansfeldtphotography.com
Twitter: @GEMPhoto326

Giliane's lifework focuses on portraying women as strong and independent. She hopes that through her photography, she can dismantle the notion of "The Frail Woman." Ultimately, she stands to challenge norms and unmask the power of the feminine.

Shannon Tacheny
photographer
651.489.8281
featherbluestudios.com

Shannon Tacheny is owner of Feather Blue Studios. She specializes in portrait, fashion, and commercial photography in-studio or throughout the Twin Cities. Her style is fresh, fun, and vibrant.

Additionally, we would like to thank those who helped us with this guide in many important ways: Elijah and Jackie Parker and Sonoma Swanson.

Index

By Category

By Category (continued)

By Category (continued)

By Neighborhood

By Neighborhood (continued)

By Neighborhood (continued)